LEARNING OBJECTIVES FOR INDIVIDUALIZED INSTRUCTION

LANGUAGE ARTS

Westinghouse Learning Press
Division of Westinghouse Learning Corporation

Library of Congress Card Catalog Number 75-23425

ISBN 0-88250-777-X (Softcover Edition)
ISBN 0-88250-772-9 (Hardcover Edition)

Westinghouse Learning Press
770 Lucerne Drive
Sunnyvale, California 94086

Division of Westinghouse Learning Corporation
New York, New York 10017

Printed in the United States of America

Text set in 10 point Zenith with display
lines in 13 point Goudy Heavyface

Cover design and art by Steven Jacobs Design,
Palo Alto, California

Editorial and production by Westinghouse
Learning Press, Sunnyvale, California

Composition by Typothetae, Palo Alto, California

Lithography by George Banta Company,
Menasha, Wisconsin

Contents

Objectives from the following Westinghouse Learning Press publications have been used or adapted with permission of the authors.

Biology: An Individualized Course
Robert N. Hurst, David H. McGaw, Kenneth H. Bush, Curtis L. Smiley

Earth Science: An Individualized Course
Joseph C. Gould, Charles J. Mott, N. Gerald Langford

Algebra: An Individualized Course
Ephraim G. Salins, Russell L. Fleury

American Government: An Individualized Course
Wallace P. Harrison

Sociology: An Individualized Course, First Edition and Revised Edition
Robert A. Butler

Psychology: An Individualized Course, First Edition and Revised Edition
Richard L. Morgan

Economics: An Individualized Course
Dayton Y. Roberts, Alfred J. Furnweger

English Composition: An Individualized Course, First Edition and Revised Edition
Benson R. Schulman

A Curse on Confusion: An Individualized Approach to Clear Writing
Lowell A. Draper

The Relevance of Patterns: An Individualized Approach to Writing Improvement
Lucille M. Thomas

The Relevance of Sound: An Individualized Approach to Phonetic and Structural Analysis
Frances Coolidge

The Relevance of Words: An Individualized Approach to Spelling
David J. Peterson

The Relevance of Listening: An Individualized Course
Harold D. Sartain

AC Circuits/DC Circuits: An Individualized Approach to Electronics
Paul E. Trejo

Toward Instructional Accountability: A Practical Guide to Educational Change
John E. Roueche, Barton R. Herrscher

Computer Programming: An Individualized Course in FORTRAN IV
Carl A. Grame, Daniel J. O'Donnell

Introduction

Westinghouse Learning Corporation has been involved for almost ten years in developing individualized instructional material for kindergarten, elementary school, high school, college, career training, and industry. Since objectives are a basic component of individualized learning, Westinghouse Learning Corporation has necessarily been a leader in formulating objectives.

With increasing demands for accountability in teaching, many teachers and instructors have found a need for objectives to use or to adapt for their courses. Others wanted guidelines so that they could develop their own objectives as they moved toward greater individualization and accountability in teaching.

This set of objectives has been produced to provide learning objectives for an age range quite different from the usual grade levels, particularly for the mature student, who may never have mastered objectives that are ordinarily covered in earlier years. The typical grade-level organization is not appropriate for these students, who may need some very basic elements but are nonetheless ready to explore the disciplines at a comparatively sophisticated level.

Most of these objectives have been used with students, particularly in classes that emphasize individualization as well as in learning centers and resource laboratories that concentrate on a diagnostic and remedial approach to basic skills.

Cognitive Levels

In the first Westinghouse Learning Corporation collection, *Behavioral Objectives,* the keying of objectives to cognitive levels based on Bloom's *Taxonomy of Educational Objectives, Cognitive Domain,* was so successful that this system has been used again, with some adaptations. Determining the cognitive level of objectives necessarily involves a degree of subjectivity, but every effort has been made to reduce subjectivity through use of a chart, listing the verbs that seem appropriate for behavior at the various cognitive levels. Often modifiers of these verbs have had to be added. Where questions arose regarding the cognitive level of the objectives in these volumes, the editors made judgments as to the actual performance involved, based on the following questions that help to define the six basic levels.

I. Are the students asked simply to repeat facts or show that they have memorized something?
II. Do students have to show understanding of the information presented?
III. Must students apply knowledge to a new situation (as in problem solving), or must they make predictions?
IV. Is it necessary to analyze and organize information?
V. Does the objective require combining and presenting information in a new or creative way?
VI. Do students have to draw together several cognitive levels in evaluating the material or in making judgments based on evaluation?

Using these six questions as the framework, the editors developed the chart on pages viii–ix, which lists verbs that have been used for each of the cognitive levels.

A major difficulty in assigning levels arises from the confusion between the *kinds* of cognitive activity and the *content* associated with that activity. For example, to the student in medical school, a large amount of cognitive activity may be of the kind that is often referred to as the lowest level, memorization. Anatomical terms, drug dosages, symptoms, and treatments must be memorized. The content level of this activity is extremely high, but the activity itself remains at level I. A conscious effort has been made in this collection to present objectives that cover a broad spectrum of cognitive levels and content. It is up to the user of these books to transform a given objective to meet either the content or the cognitive level that is appropriate for a particular unit of instruction.

Organization

Beyond the major divisions into four volumes—Language Arts, Mathematics, Science, and Social Science—a broad set of subject classifications has been used. No attempt has been made to provide comprehensive subject coverage, and many objectives in one category are also applicable to another. The comprehensive index provides cross referencing. Although there are subject subdivisions, there is no grade-level designation. When any text is made up of small parts, the constraints of print mean that each item has a fixed position on a page and within a volume—a position that establishes a sequential relationship regardless of whether such a relationship is logical or intentional. Since objectives may potentially be sequenced in many ways, it is important to understand that the arrangement of this collection is not intended to suggest any prescriptive order. In the sections emphasizing skills, there is some natural sequence based on the cumulative nature of some skills, but in subject areas topics may be presented in almost any order.

In *Learning Objectives for Individualized Instruction,* terminal objectives have been established to provide appropriate learning segments. These terminal objectives are numbered and printed in boldface.

Subobjectives, which may be called transitional or enabling objectives, contribute to the mastery of a terminal objective. These transitional objectives may appear as part of more than one terminal objective. Transitional objectives and terminal objectives are both assigned cognitive levels; transitional objectives are never given a higher cognitive level than the terminal objectives with which they are associated.

The Numbering System

Because many instructors wish to use the computer for storage and retrieval of objectives and related test items, each terminal objective has been given a numerical designator. These numbers have been set up as follows. The two digits at the far left indicate a major area: 01, Language Arts; 02, Mathematics; 03, Social Science; 04, Science. Career areas and other major areas can be added, up to 99. The three middle digits have been reserved for subject areas; in this collection numbers have been assigned to subject areas at intervals of five to allow for interpolation of such other subjects as an instructor finds appropriate. The three digits on the right in the numerical designator signify terminal objectives; these have also been spaced at intervals of five so that others may be inserted.

Since courses have not yet been developed in all subject areas, some disciplines are not covered in this collection and there has been no effort to make coverage complete within a subject area. This collection is designed to encourage the instructor to use these volumes as guidelines rather than as a definite set. Every instructor should feel free to add, subtract, and adapt objectives to meet individual, class, and institutional needs.

Levels of Learning Objectives

I KNOWLEDGE	II COMPREHENSION	III APPLICATION
Emphasis: Recall	*Emphasis:* Grasp of meaning, intent, or relationship	*Emphasis:* Applying appropriate principles or generalizations
choose from a list (judgment not involved) define (give a dictionary definition) fill in the blank (or complete) follow directions identify indicate label list locate (on a map or a given document) match name select (judgment not involved)	classify define (in student's own words) describe explain express in other terms find (as in math) measure paraphrase put in order recognize rewrite simplify suggest summarize trace (on a map, chart, etc.) *Math* add (find the sum) balance calculate compute (using a given formula) divide (find the quotient) factor find square root or raise to power multiply (find the product) perform operations on numbers subtract (find the difference)	apply collect information (supply correct equation or formula) compute construct convert (in math) draw determine (calculate) demonstrate derive differentiate between discuss distinguish between expand express in a discussion estimate find (implies investigation) interpret investigate illustrate (give examples not previously specified) graph keep records locate (information) make participate perform (except in math or in public) plan predict (from known factors) prepare present prove (in math) solve (problems expressed in words) use trace (development, history, process) translate

Levels of Learning Objectives (continued)

IV ANALYSIS	V SYNTHESIS	VI EVALUATION
Emphasis: Breaking into constituent parts and detecting relationships of the parts and the way they are organized and organizing material according to a coherent pattern	*Emphasis:* Putting together elements or parts to form a whole that reflects originality	*Emphasis:* On values, making qualitative or quantitative judgment, using criteria from internal or external sources and standards
analyze compare and contrast criticize debate deduce determine differentiate between (by analysis) draw conclusions formulate form generalizations make inferences organize relate (show relationships)	combine and organize design devise develop perform (in public) produce present (an original report or work) write (an original composition)	choose (based on evaluation) decide evaluate judge make a decision

This collection would not be possible without the cooperation of the following:

Science: Robert N. Hurst, Purdue University, Lafayette, Indiana; Kenneth H. Bush, David H. McGaw, and Curtis L. Smiley, West Lafayette High School, West Lafayette, Indiana; Joseph C. Gould, Charles J. Mott, and N. Gerald Langford, St. Petersburg Junior College, Clearwater, Florida; Miles H. Anderson, University of California, Los Angeles, California; Paul E. Trejo, De Anza College, Cupertino, California

Mathematics: Ephraim G. Salins, Montgomery College, Takoma Park, Maryland; Russell L. Fleury, University of Maryland, College Park, Maryland; Carl A. Grame and Daniel J. O'Donnell, De Anza College, Cupertino, California

Social Science: Wallace P. Harrison, Los Angeles Pierce College, Los Angeles, California; Robert A. Butler, Louisburg College, Louisburg, North Carolina; Richard L. Morgan, Mitchell College, Statesville, North Carolina; Dayton Y. Roberts, Texas Tech University, Lubbock, Texas; Alfred J. Furnweger, Santa Fe Community College, Gainesville, Florida; John E. Roueche, University of Texas, Austin, Texas; Barton R. Herrscher, College Associates, Austin, Texas; Rita and Stuart Johnson, School of Medicine, University of North Carolina, Chapel Hill, North Carolina; Marcia H. Perlstein, Opportunity II High School, San Francisco, California

Language Arts: Benson R. Schulman, Los Angeles Pierce College, Los Angeles, California; Lowell A. Draper, Modesto Community College, Modesto, California; Lucille M. Thomas, Grand Rapids Junior College, Grand Rapids, Michigan; Frances Coolidge, De Anza College, Cupertino, California; David J. Peterson, San Jose Unified School District, San Jose, California; Harold D. Sartain, Des Moines Area Community College, Ankeny, Iowa

Further acknowledgment is made to all who participated in developing objectives for Project PLAN* and *Behavioral Objectives: A Guide to Individualizing Learning*.

The Editors
Westinghouse Learning Press
Sunnyvale, California
15 September 1975

LANGUAGE ARTS

Listening and Speaking

01-005-005 **Given short listening passages, recall details and the order of their presentation. I**

Recall details from short lists of information presented to you orally. I

Recall the order of presentation of details presented in an oral passage. I

01-005-010 **Given short listening passages, recognize and recall relationships and unifying elements. II**

From oral passages identify and recall relationships of size, length, position, and arrangement. I

Recognize unity in short lists of information presented orally. II

01-005-015 **Given short listening passages, recognize and recall sequence and patterns. II**

Recognize and recall sequence of items in a series presented orally. II

Recognize and recall patterned relationships in short series and groups of information in oral passages. II

01-005-020 **In a situation dependent on following oral directions, perform as the directions specify. III**

Recognize assumptions in oral directions. II

Recognize and make inferences about oral directions. II

List and use specific skills related to following directions, including the elements listed below. III
1. Having required materials at hand
2. Following directions in recommended sequence
3. Asking for clarification or repetition
4. Attending to requests concerning paper headings, numbering, and form

5. Making accurate changes in test items as called for
6. Taking notes as permitted and needed
7. Considering directions and suggestions about evaluation of responses
8. Marking responses and writing answers as designated
9. Attending to examples and sample items
10. Attending to and observing time limits
11. Noting instructor's advice and emphasis

01-005-025 **Understand and apply the skills necessary to building listening comprehension, and demonstrate comprehension by taking accurate notes. III**

List three ways that are useful in concentrating attention. I

Describe your listening purpose in relation to each of several oral passages. II

Given an oral passage, demonstrate that you can review the information mentally by presenting a précis, summary, or outline. III

Relate speech speed and thought speed, and discuss how the difference can contribute to listening skills. III

Discuss the problems related to coordination of listening with eye and hand movements. III

Relate elements like charts, maps, and diagrams to an oral passage. III

Demonstrate your ability to listen selectively by presenting a one-sentence summary of an oral passage that includes several speakers. III

List transitional words and devices, and describe how each helps a listener follow idea development. II

Prepare notes from a variety of listening passages related to different subject areas. III

Recognize rhetorical devices, and describe your own emotional reaction to such devices in a given listening passage. II

01-005-030   Apply a variety of techniques to improve your understanding of oral directions.   III

Recall details from short oral directions.   I

Recall the sequence of details.   II

Recognize, recall, and use directional cues and reference points.   III

Identify and use visual cues that accompany oral directions.   I

Recognize emphasis on key words and phrases.   I

Recognize relationships among individual items.   II

Follow directions in the specified sequence.   III

Make elementary inferences from details.   III

01-005-035   In oral passages of several paragraphs, recognize subdivisions of the main idea and their sequence and arrangement.   II

Identify subdivisions of the main idea in a short talk.   I

Recognize sequence and arrangement in an oral message.   II

01-005-040   Recognize the organization of a given oral passage.   II

Recognize methods of developing main ideas.   II

Connect main ideas with their supporting ideas.   II

Recognize patterns of organization of information in oral messages.   II

01-005-045   Relate speaker's point of view to content in a talk.   IV

Recognize assumptions about the content of short talks.   II

Make inferences about a speaker's or an author's point of view. IV

01-005-050 **Given oral passages of several paragraphs, recognize and recall details and main ideas. II**

Recall details from short talks and oral readings. II

Recognize and recall main ideas of short oral passages. II

01-005-055 **Given oral passages of several paragraphs, recognize elements of unity and relationships between details and the main idea. II**

Recognize unity among individual parts of short talks. II

Identify relationships between details and the main idea. I

01-005-060 **Develop criteria for evaluating content and speech techniques, and use these techniques in evaluating oral presentations. VI**

Evaluate the performance of a moderator in a discussion with respect to giving evidence of being well prepared on the discussion topic, asking questions that start a discussion and keep it moving, withholding personal opinion, keeping the discussion to the point and pacing the discussion, bringing the discussion to a conclusion within the allotted time, and summarizing what was discovered or learned during the discussion. VI

In writing and/or discussion, analyze both written and oral presentations for faulty generalizations. IV

01-005-065 **Differentiate between appropriate and inappropriate forms of conversation. V**

Identify the basic elements of courtesy that are desirable in person-to-person conversations, group conversations, and telephone conversations. I

Differentiate between acceptable and unacceptable conversations, and develop guidelines for improving your own conversation. V

Describe the differences in levels of conversation between two people and within a group. II

01-005-070 Prepare an organized oral report. III

Apply the skill of sequencing to organize material for an oral presentation. III

After reading several references on a chosen topic, prepare a project that includes a visual model and present a discussion of the topic. III

Prepare an oral report, using the following steps. III
1. Choose and limit a subject.
2. Locate information.
3. Take notes.
4. Organize the notes in three sections: one that leads into, one that expands, and one that summarizes the topic.
5. Prepare the report.

01-005-075 Present an organized oral report. III

Present a five-minute talk on a topic of your choice. III

Give an oral presentation of an original project or a book review. III

After reading an account of a scientific adventure, present an oral report related to the adventure. III

Given a controversial topic, make an oral presentation in which you try to persuade others to agree with your point of view. III

01-005-080 Evaluate the techniques used by a speaker in an oral presentation. VI

Analyze the content of the following parts of an oral presentation: the speaker's purpose, clarity of information, organization of the material. IV

Evaluate the following parts of a speaker's delivery of an oral presentation: clarity and voice control, posture and action, eye contact with the audience. VI

Develop a checklist of points to use in evaluating a speaker. V

01-005-085 Present a speech, using appropriate techniques. III

Demonstrate voicing techniques in a speech by varying the pitch, volume, and forcefulness of your voice and the rate at which you speak. You should also exercise proper articulation and pronunciation. III

Demonstrate body action and gesture as a means of communication in a speech. III

Demonstrate in a speech at least two methods of eliciting a response from your audience. III

Given a choice of topic, related materials, and a list of procedures, select and present a five-minute speech, demonstrating voicing techniques. III

Present an oral explanation in which you include some form of visual aid. The explanation should be understandable to an audience that is unfamiliar with the topic. III

Given a situation in which you are asked to explain how to get from one place to another, present clear directions. They must contain adequate information and be arranged in the proper sequence. III

Prepare an oral presentation about a personal experience. III

Prepare and present a brief speech in which you introduce a speaker to an audience; include the speaker's name, the speech title, and the speaker's background, including place of birth, education, previous jobs held, present status or position, committees served on, articles or books written, and personal facts of possible interest to the audience. III

01-005-090   **Produce one of the following forms of nonverbal communication—painting, sculpture, drawing, collage, photograph, movie—to express a feeling, an attitude, or an idea on a specific category. V**

Given three means of nonverbal communication (pictures, objects, and gestures) and an idea to communicate, predict the ease or difficulty, and the effectiveness, of each. III

Using symbols that you have found or developed, visually communicate an idea or feeling to another person so that person can state the idea or feeling verbally. III

Develop visual signs that communicate information to large groups of people. V

Use skills of nonverbal communication in a speech. III

Find an art print, picture, or photograph on a topic of your choice, and explain how your example illustrates that topic. II

Develop an original project that expresses your feeling about a specific category in literature. V

Investigate what psychologists say about body language as nonverbal communication, and present an original skit that illustrates some examples of body language. V

01-005-095   **Participate in achieving the goals of a discussion group. III**

Review the guidelines for a discussion that apply to the participant in a discussion group. I

Review group-discussion techniques by expressing your point of view on a topic from your reading in a specific category. II

After reading two selections from a reading list on a specific category, discuss the category, citing examples from your reading. III

Review group discussion techniques by participating in an open-ended group discussion in which no one solution is apparent. Define the topic, contribute relevant ideas, contribute to the resolution of the problem, and state whether or not you think your contribution was worthwhile.   III

01-005-100   Apply techniques for leading a discussion, and evaluate the result.   VI

Describe the rules that should be followed by the leader of a discussion group.   II

Evaluate the technique used by a discussion leader according to the following criteria.   VI
1. Introducing the topic under discussion
2. Refraining from giving personal views
3. Deciding who is to speak
4. Keeping the discussion moving on the topic
5. Giving everyone a chance to speak
6. Summarizing the main points

Demonstrate your ability to lead a discussion group.   III

01-005-105   Participate in group situations in which personal opinions and values are being expressed, and evaluate the outcome of such a situation.   VI

Participate in a discussion by showing that you can prepare yourself on the subject so your contributions are worthwhile, participate in a discussion without monopolizing or interrupting, be tactful in your comments, and avoid making comments of little consequence or dwelling on irrelevant ideas.   III

Participate in a debate on any subject of current interest as debater, moderator, or evaluator. An acceptable debate will contain the following.   III
1. Evidence that is definite, extensive, pertinent, and convincing
2. Organization that is clear, logical, and strong
3. Analysis that shows a thorough study of the question
4. Refutation that shows the speaker is able to adapt as well as answer and think clearly
5. Delivery that is enhanced by one's personal appearance, voice, articulation, and deportment

Demonstrate debating procedures by participating in a debate on a personal or social issue. III

Participate in a panel discussion as speaker, moderator, or evaluator. When participating in a panel discussion, remember the following points. III
1. Research the topic.
2. Plan some of the contributions you are to make.
3. Speak in an informal, conversational manner.
4. Speak in a strong, clear voice.
5. Don't let one person talk too much, and don't let long periods of silence occur.

Participate in a role-playing situation in which people are trying to achieve a specific purpose, with one person obviously contributing to or detracting from the achievement of the group. III

Develop a checklist for evaluating participation in a group where divergent views are presented. V

01-005-110 **Explain the probable source of power in situations where a group or an individual has power over another group or individual. II**

Given situations of human group behavior, describe examples of the following characteristics of groups: goals (immediate and/or long-range), the patterns of roles and status in the group, the norms or the generally accepted standard of behavior recognized by group members. II

Given situations of human group behavior in which one or more of the following types of conflicts occur, state the probable sequences of the conflict, propose alternate solutions to remove the conflict, and after evaluating the plans, select one that would provide the most appropriate solution. II
1. Conflicts about group goals
2. Conflicts about role behavior (differences in role expectations)
3. Conflicts about group norms

01-005-115   **Use logic and rhetoric in discussing topics and in presenting oral arguments or debates.   V**

Recognize the irrelevant statements in a given written passage.   II

Given written passages in which the following techniques are used, recognize each technique.   II
1. Progressive refinement of a core statement
2. High verb density
3. Linking and transitional expressions
4. Repetition of phrasal or clausal structure
5. Metaphor
6. Imagery
7. Relation of sentence pattern to content

Using inductive logic, support an argument for a given statement.   III

Given two statements of a syllogism, write a third statement that completes the syllogism.   III

Determine valid deductive arguments (syllogisms) and invalid ones, and identify the source(s) of the fallacies.   IV

Given passages of argument, determine the main ideas and the patterns of logic (induction, deduction, analogy) that they contain and determine their logical validity.   IV

Analyze given statements as judgments of fact, as inferences, or as value judgments.   IV

Make inferences derived from a given paragraph.   IV

Given a list of patterns for solving problems, suggest which patterns might be used to solve specified problems.   II

Develop a report on an assigned topic, using several rhetorical strategies and several patterns of logic.   V

Given a list of propositions, determine whether they are arguable or nonarguable.   IV

Given a list of arguable propositions, determine which ones are propositions of fact and which are propositions of action. IV

Given an arguable or major proposition, suggest at least five minor propositions or arguments to support it. II

Given evidence in support of an arguable proposition, determine which evidence is fact and which is opinion. IV

01-005-120 **Discuss the range of expression in an oral presentation. III**

In written form or in a discussion, suggest how tonal qualities in speaking can affect the meaning of words and the rendition projected to an audience. III

Practice and present a five-minute reading of a prose selection to be judged on volume, rate, pitch, gestures, body movements, and mood changes. III

Present a reading of three poems, either written by the same person or related in theme, as well as an introduction and transitional remarks. III

In an oral reading offer an interpretation of two poems of your choice by the same author. III

Present an excerpt of dialog between two people in a play, using a different voice to represent each character. III

Present an oral reading of a scene from *Julius Caesar,* and give examples from that scene of a least six of the following features: puns, blank verse, prose speeches, run-on lines, end-stopped lines, rhyming couplets, repetition, metaphors, similes. III

01-005-125 **Develop dramatic techniques by combining concepts, principles, and generalizations. V**

Identify important guidelines for participating in a play. I

Given a skit that has been prepared, present the skit to to the class.   III

Summarize information that should be included when writing a script for a skit.   II

Write a script for a play that includes a list of characters, the setting of each scene, and dialog with speakers' actions.   V

Participate in a play that has been written by you or by a classmate.   III

Word Skills

01-010-005   **Recognize the importance of auditory discrimination and audiovisual association, and apply these skills in reading and spelling unfamiliar words. III**

From a list of word pairs like the following, circle the parts in each pair that sound different, and indicate whether those sounds occur in the beginning, in the middle, or at the end of the words. I

1. corner, cornet
2. censor, center
3. climate, climax
4. tension, mention
5. detain, retain
6. extent, extend
7. devil, level
8. divide, divine
9. protect, project
10. florid, floret
11. bantam, phantom
12. flower, glower
13. founder, sounder
14. garble, gargle

Show your understanding of consonant blends and consonant digraphs by giving several examples of each. II

From a word list like the following, presented orally, indicate the number of syllables in each word: *pendant, pandemonium, nerve, birch, somnolent, demise, osmosis, omnipotent, coerce, proletarian, oboe, corpulent.* I

In a list of words like the following, indicate the syllable with the primary accent: *magnanimous, pertinacious, masochistic, perpendicular, metabolism, omnipotent, sarcophagus, anachronism, plutocracy, somnambulate.* I

Given a list of words like the following, indicate which pairs rhyme. I

1. expel, gazelle
2. learn, return
3. guest, impressed
4. launch, hunch
5. braille, appeal
6. germane, champagne
7. beguile, compile
8. intense, expanse
9. kept, slipped
10. convince, enhance
11. persuade, arcade
12. opaque, forsake
13. taste, priest

Recognize short vowel sounds and long vowel sounds, and give examples of words that contain each of these sounds.   II

Recognize the schwa (ə) sound and its various representations (*a, e, i, o, u*), and give examples of each.   II

Recognize consonant-vowel digraphs, and give examples of word sounds that involve the sounds of these combinations.   II

Recognize vowel diphthongs in words that contain these vowel combinations.   II

Recognize initial, middle, and ending sounds that involve consonants, blends, and vowels.   II

01-010-010   Given a chart of graphemic–phonemic relationships, analyze your own misspelled words to determine the patterns of your spelling problems.   IV

Recognize the different ways in which a given sound is represented by symbols.   II

Define the terms *grapheme* and *phoneme*.   II

Define the processes of decoding and encoding, and use these processes in reading and spelling.   III

01-010-015   Apply skills of phonetic and structural analysis to improve your spelling and reading.   IV

Using a list of at least thirty words that you have at some time misspelled, design at least three methods or systems for mastering the spelling of these words.   IV

Apply spelling rules for words in which the final consonant is doubled before a suffix is added.   III

Given orally words that end in *-sede, -ceed,* and *-cede,* write sentences in which you use and spell the words correctly.   III

Given a list of some of the most frequently misused and misspelled words and phrases, read, use, and spell them correctly.   III

Describe the meanings of the verb suffixes *-ize, -fy* (or *-ify*), *-ate,* and *-en,* and use the verb suffixes to form words.   III

Use the verb prefixes *en-, em-, be-,* and *re-* to form new words.   III

Spell correctly, using the following as guides: pronunciation; rules of prefixes, suffixes, and other rules; the dictionary.   III

01-010-020   **Using a chart of phonetic symbols for reference, translate both oral and written passages into phonetic symbols, and read aloud such passages translated by others.   III**

Given a chart of phonetic symbols for reference, translate a short oral passage into phonetic symbols.   III

With a chart of symbols as a reference, translate a short written passage into phonetic symbols.   III

Using a chart of symbols as a guide, read aloud a passage.   III

01-010-025   **In reading unfamiliar words, apply structural-analysis techniques related to affixes and roots to recognize meaning.   III**

Review structural analysis by finding clues to the meaning of a word by recognizing its parts—root, prefix, or suffix.   II

Review structural analysis by recognizing the following structures of grammatical significance.   II
1. Endings: *-ed, -ing, -s, -er, -est*
2. Plurals: *-s, -es, -ies, -ves* (and variants)

Given a group of sentences in which one word in each sentence is incomplete, and given a list of suffixes and prefixes, select the appropriate affix to complete the word.   II

Recognize the rules for adding affixes to roots.   II

Divide words according to the rules of syllabication.   III

01-010-030   Use a dictionary to identify the structure and meaning of words.   III

Use a sample dictionary page to find an example of the following: guide word, entry word, pronunciation key, definitions.   III

Given a list of entry words, use guide words to locate each entry word in a dictionary.   III

Given a list of derived words that are not entry words, use the dictionary to locate the base (root) word. Use the meaning of the base (root) word and the affixes to suggest the meaning of the derived word.   III

Find prefix and suffix entries in the dictionary. Use the entries to form new words.   III

Given a group of sentences, each of which contains a word that has the same spelling but a different meaning in each sentence, locate in a dictionary the definition of the word as it is used in each sentence.   III

Use a dictionary to find the correct meaning of words given in context.   III

Use a dictionary to find the meanings of common idioms.   III

Use a dictionary to find the syllables, pronunciation, parts of speech, meaning, and synonyms for a given word.   III

Referring to a dictionary, use hyphens with compound words and numbers correctly.   III

Recognize that words are divided into syllables differently for pronunciation and hyphenation.   II

01-010-035   Use a variety of techniques to infer meanings of unfamiliar words.   III

Use context clues as a way of inferring meanings of unfamiliar words.   III

Use related words and roots as a way of inferring meanings of unfamiliar words. III

Use the meanings of prefixes and suffixes as a way of inferring meanings of unfamiliar words. III

Given a pair of homonyms, define each homonym. I

Given a list of words, recognize the words that are similar in meaning. II

Given a word, identify its antonym. I

Given an incomplete analogy and a list of words, recognize the word that completes the analogy. II

Given the first half of several different kinds of word analogies, recognize another pair of words that are analogous in the same way that the words in the first pair are. II

Given a sentence that contains a malapropism (a word that sounds somewhat like the one intended), recognize the malapropism and replace it with the correct word. II

Present the meaning of common words in two of these ways: a formal definition, a synonym, a definition by contrast, a working definition. II

Given words of identical or somewhat similar pronunciation, distinguish their meanings and uses. II

Given words of identical or somewhat similar pronunciation, recognize the word to be used in a given sentence. II

In written and oral work, demonstrate ability to use the correct forms of *sit, set, lie, lay, learn,* and *teach.* III

In written and oral work, demonstrate ability to use the correct forms of *tear, wear, fall,* and *swim.* III

Given a word or group of words in context, recognize the following context clues related to those words: definition, explanation, opposite idea, example. II

Infer meanings of the technical vocabulary in a given scientific selection. III

Use words with an understanding of levels of usage (appropriateness), idiomatic use of prepositions, concrete versus abstract words, clichés, jargon, and simplicity. III

Distinguish the difference in meaning between closely related words, and give examples from personal observation. III

01-010-040 **Explain the meanings of common prefixes, suffixes, and roots derived from other languages, and use this information to infer the meanings of unfamiliar words. III**

Show your understanding of prefixes by deriving the meaning of words. II

Give the meaning of each of the following prefixes of opposition, and give examples of words that derive a part of their meaning from each prefix: *anti-, contra-, counter-, non-, un-, in-, mis-.* III

Give the meaning of each of the following prefixes of separation, and give examples of words that derive a part of their meaning from each prefix: *ab-, de-, dis-, ex-* or *ec-, se-.* III

For each of the following prefixes, give an example of a word that derives part of its meaning from the prefix: *ad-, inter-, post-, pre-, ante-, pre-, re-, sub-, trans-, tele-, intro-, ob-, per-.* III

For each of the following prefixes, give an example of a word that derives a part of its meaning from the prefix: *circum-, peri, con-, com-, co-, sym-, syn-, lux-, luc-, photo-, magni-, mega-, multi-, poly-, omni-, pan(to)-, prim-, proto-, super-, ultra-, hyper-.* III

Define each of the following numerical prefixes, and give an example of each as used in a word: *uni-, mono-, semi-, hemi-, demi-, sept-, hept(a)-, cent(i)-, quin-, pent (a)-, du(o)-, bi-, tri-, quad-, tetra-, octo-, octa-, sex-, hex(a)-, dec(a)-, mill(i, e)-.* I

Describe the origins of words by giving examples of prefixes and roots and the relation of these parts to the meaning of the words. III

Find examples of English words derived from roots like the following: *gamos* (marriage), *psyche* (life, soul), *pseudo* (false), *nemesis* (retribution), *narcissus* (self-love), *nautilus* (sailor), *bellum* (belligerent), *loqui* (to speak), *corpus* (body), *octo* (eight), *vulcan* (fire, metal working), *ped* (foot). III

01-010-045   Trace the history of a word as a linguistic form. III

Given a list of English words, find their meanings and the meanings of related words from the root of the original word. II

Given a list of words, identify words that are borrowed from a language other than English. II

Given two columns of words, match words from one column with the appropriate words from the other column to form compound words. I

Give an example of each of the following sources of words: slang, blended words, words formed by combining the first letter of each word of a phrase, words derived from names of famous people. II

Explain the increased use of slang and its influence on language. II

Recognize new words that are formed from existing elements to meet new needs. II

Explain the effect of technology on the English language. II

Recognize the ways in which dialects differ. II

Explain how vocabulary choices are influenced by age, sex, education, occupation, and origin. II

Identify "Americanisms" that have entered the English language, and give examples of each type. II

List methods by which new "Americanisms" are being coined, and give examples of relatively new words for each method you name.   II

01-010-050   **Explain and give examples of regional, ethnic, and dialectical differences in vocabulary, pronunciation, and syntax.   III**

Discuss how United States regional dialects change in relation to population movement, geographical isolation, and economic development.   III

Given a list of words, recognize those that have the same meaning but are formed from different dialects.   II

Explain how the relationship between the English colonies and the Mother Country (later the United States and Great Britain) is reflected in the use of the English language in the United States during the seventeenth, eighteenth, nineteenth, and twentieth centuries.   II

Describe and list examples of at least six regional differences in vocabulary, pronunciation, or syntax.   III

Describe and list examples of at least six ethnic or dialectal differences in vocabulary, pronunciation, or syntax.   III

01-010-055   **Given samples of oral and written language, describe the differences of patterns and make judgments regarding the acceptability of these samples in varied social, educational, and career situations.   VI**

Recognize and give examples of pronunciation, vocabulary, and syntax difference between oral and written language.   III

Explain what is meant by "nonstandard speech patterns," tell whether you agree or disagree that such patterns exist, and (if you think they do exist) suggest ways of overcoming them.   II

Define *standard English* and *nonstandard English,* and describe how these definitions affect you in a social context and an academic situation.   II

01-010-060   Define the term inflection, and use inflectional rules as they relate to English.   III

Define the term *morpheme.*   II

Given a list of singular nouns, write each noun in the plural form.   II

Given a list of noun phrases, write the possessive form for each phrase.   II

Relate person and number to inflected verb endings.   I

List the present-tense form of a given verb.   I

List the past-tense forms of regular verbs.   I

List the past-tense forms of irregular verbs.   I

List the principal parts of regular and irregular verbs.   I

Rewrite given verbs as present participles.   II

Use comparative and superlative morphemes.   III

Distinguish between confusing pairs of words like *lie, lay* and *set, sit* in all tense forms.   III

Construct nouns from verbs + *er.* Differentiate an adjective + comparatives from a verb + *er.*   III

Make adjectives out of certain nouns by adding -*ful* to them. Use the adjectives in sentences.   III

Make nouns of measurement out of certain nouns by adding -*ful* to them, and use the nouns in sentences.   III

Construct abstract nouns by adding the morpheme -*ness* to adjectives.   III

Construct adjectives by adding the morpheme -*less* to certain nouns.   III

01-010-065   Classify words as they function in sentences, distinguishing nouns, verbs, adjectives, and adverbs.   II

Identify verbs by their ability to indicate action or state of being.   I

Identify and write single-word verbs, verbals, and verb phrases.   II

Recognize verb tenses, and distinguish verbs from verbals and adverbs.   II

Distinguish verb phrases from verbs.   II

Identify participles, auxiliaries, and adverbs.   I

01-010-070   Analyze the relationship of emotional and psychological impact of words to semantics.   IV

Given two or more words having the same primary meaning (denotation), suggest an implied or secondary meaning (connotation) for each word.   II

Given a word that is neutral in association, suggest two synonymous words or phrases—one that is favorable in association and one that is unfavorable.   II

Rewrite a given passage, replacing selected terms with more specific terms that fit the context of the passage.   II

Classify sentences and passages as colloquial, uneducated, or formal expressions.   II

Given a list of figurative expressions, recognize the expressions that give a fresh interpretation of human experience.   II

Given a passage that includes unnecessary words and phrases, rewrite it in the most condensed and economical form possible.   II

Describe each of the following terms as it relates to the study of semantics. II

1. Referent	12. Inference
2. Verbal	13. Logic
3. Nonverbal	14. Levels of abstraction
4. Semantically safe	15. Value judgment
5. Verifiable	16. Color words
6. Emotive	17. Propaganda
7. Subjective	18. Literacy
8. Objective	19. Denotation
9. Affective	20. Connotation
10. Analogy	21. Communication
11. Generalization	

Analyze written statements as to whether or not their words are at a level of abstraction too high to communicate a clear message. IV

Given the picture of a particular event and a statement that is a value judgment of the event, rewrite the statement so that it expresses only what is semantically safe to express. III

Recognize written examples of each of the following semantic fallacies: unverifiable referent, false analogy, color words, overgeneralization, confusing facts with inference, confusing facts with value judgment. II

Sentence Skills

01-015-005   **Write sentences, using the basic parts of speech.   III**

Recognize nouns, verbs, adjectives, and adverbs by their use in sentences.   II

Identify the plural of a given singular noun.   I

List the singular possessive and plural possessive forms of nouns.   I

Recognize predicate nouns or linking-verb complements.   II

Demonstrate the use of noun markers in written work.   III

Write sentences using personal pronouns as subjects and as linking-verb complements.   III

Write the singular, past, and participial forms of regular and irregular verbs, and use each form in a sentence.   III

Write sentences, using the comparative and superlative forms of adjectives, including the irregular forms of *good, bad, many,* and *little.*   III

Write sentences using personal pronouns as direct objects.   III

Write sentences using possessive pronouns.   III

Write sentences using indefinite pronouns as substitutes for nouns.   III

Write sentences using verbs that involve auxiliaries.   III

Write the plain, singular, past, and participial forms of regular and irregular verbs, and use each form in a sentence.   III

Write sentences using comparative and superlative forms of adverbs.   III

Write sentences using adjectives that come before nouns. III

Write sentences using predicate adjectives (complements). III

Recognize prepositions and objects of prepositions in sentences. II

Given sentences in which prepositional phrases have been improperly placed, rewrite the sentences correctly. II

Write sentences using connectives other than the connectives used for compounding. III

Write sentences using interjections. III

01-015-010   Use punctuation and capitalization appropriately in writing sentences. III

Identify errors in capitalization, punctuation, and spelling in a given business letter. I

In writing dialog and direct quotations that include broken quotations, use punctuation and capitalization appropriately. III

Given a group of sentences containing quotations that do not have any punctuation or capitalization, use appropriate punctuation and capitalization. III

Use capitalization in sentences that include titles of books, poems, songs, stories, proper names, and dialog. III

Given a written selection containing errors in punctuation and capitalization, proofread the material and make the necessary corrections. III

Use capitalization in writing proper nouns and proper adjectives. III

Given a selection containing regions of countries, trade names, and the names of documents, apply rules of capitalization. III

Given a word or words underlined in a sentence, recognize whether the word(s) should be abbreviated, hyphenated, capitalized, or left unchanged. II

01-015-015   Recognize and use appropriate internal punctuation in writing sentences. III

Write several sentences that use the comma in the following ways. III
1. To separate items in a series
2. To separate independent clauses
3. To set off introductory subordinate clauses or long introductory phrases
4. To set off such nonessential elements as names used in direct address, appositives, nonrestrictive participial phrases and nonrestrictive clauses, and parenthetical expressions
5. To separate the items in dates and addresses

Write a compound sentence punctuated by a semicolon. Write a sentence that illustrates another use of the semicolon. III

Use the colon in two different ways, and explain its function in each. III

Use quotation marks in sentences. III

01-015-020   Write sentences by using nouns, pronouns, and determiners. III

Recognize nouns ending in s from verbs ending in s. II

Explain what determiners do for nouns. II

Identify proper nouns. I

Give examples of two types of determiners that appear with nouns. II

Describe six types of pronouns. II

Identify countable nouns and bulk-quantity nouns. I

Identify the antecedent of any pronoun in a sentence. I

In a given selection of sentences, make the pronouns and their antecedents agree.   III

01-015-025   Write sentences by using adjectives and adverbs. Distinguish between single-word adverbs and single-word adjectives.   III

Determine the positions that adjectives and adverbs take in sentences.   II

Explain the relationship of an adjective to a noun and of an adverb to a verb.   II

Show how adverbs and adjectives are used to make comparisons in a sentence.   II

Identify determiners and intensifiers, and explain their relationship to adjectives and adverbs in a sentence.   II

Distinguish adjectives from adverbs in a sentence.   I

01-015-030   Write sentences using verbs and verbals, and identify the relationships of the verbs and verbals to nouns and adverbs in the sentences.   III

Recognize verb tenses, and use them with consistency in a series of sentences.   III

Distinguish among verbs, verb phrases, verbals, and adverbs.   II

Recognize and use auxiliary verbs in sentences.   III

Show the relationship between the subject and verb in the sentences you write, and use verb forms that agree with the subject.   III

Recognize and use standard verb forms that show person and number.   III

Differentiate between a compound verb and two verbs in a compound sentence.   II

Given a sentence fragment, supply a verb, if needed, to make a complete sentence.   III

01-015-035   **Differentiate between fragments and kernel sentences, and write examples of each type. III**

Explain how you would justify the use of certain fragments. II

Distinguish between clear and unclear fragments. III

Recognize unclear prepositional-phrase fragments, verbal-phrase fragments, subordinate-clause fragments, and relative-clause fragments. II

From a given list of sentences, identify single subjects and verbs and compound subjects and verbs. I

In writing, give examples of simple sentences, compound sentences, and complex sentences. II

Write fragment sentences that emphasize an idea or create special effects and therefore may be considered acceptable in writing. III

In your reading, find examples of fragment sentences used acceptably. III

01-015-040   **Differentiate among modifiers according to their functions, and relate them to the elements they modify. III**

Write sentences with correctly related and properly positioned modifiers. III

Punctuate modifiers appropriately. II

Give examples of "dangling," "squinting," and misplaced modifiers. III

Rewrite sentences containing unclear modifiers so that the meaning is clear. III

As an aid to recognizing unclear modifiers in your own writing and the writing of others, identify unclear adjectives, adverbs, prepositional phrases, clauses, participles, and modifiers in selected material. III

01-015-045   **Distinguish between restrictive and nonrestrictive relative clauses, participles, and appositives.   III**

Identify and punctuate relative clauses, participles, and appositives, and explain why this punctuation is necessary to the sentence's meaning.   III

Explain the difference between restrictive and nonrestrictive relative clauses, participles, and appositives.   II

Identify and punctuate participles.   III

Recognize the difference between restrictive and nonrestrictive participles, and punctuate them correctly in a sentence.   II

Write clear sentences, using restrictive and nonrestrictive relative clauses, participles, and appositives.   III

01-015-050   **Explain agreement in sentences as it relates to pronoun-antecedent agreement and subject-verb agreement.   III**

Recognize the relationship between a pronoun and its antecedent.   II

Identify and correct five types of pronoun confusion and one type of unintended meaning resulting from faulty pronoun-antecedent agreement.   II

Make subjects and their verbs agree.   III

Identify and correct two kinds of unintended meaning that result from faulty subject-verb agreement.   II

Recognize when and why a verb form changes.   II

Recognize singular and plural subjects, and identify collective nouns.   II

Identify antecedents of pronouns.   I

Write sentences in which single words, phrases, and clauses are used as simple and compound subjects, and explain the verb form that agrees with each subject.   III

01-015-055   Recognize basic grammatical terms and functions, and use them in writing sentences.   III

Recognize general nouns and specific nouns.   II

Given a sentence with a noun and its modifier(s) underlined, rewrite the sentence, replacing the underlined words with a single noun that means the same thing but is more concise.   III

Write sentences that contain nouns used as subject, direct object, indirect object, subject complement (predicate nominative), and appositive.   III

Given a sentence with the verb in the passive voice, write the verb in the active voice.   III

Given a sentence with a verb and its modifier(s) underlined, rewrite the sentence, replacing the underlined words with a single verb that has the same meaning.   III

Given selected sentences, recognize transitive and intransitive verbs.   II

Recognize the following parts of speech in given sentences: noun, verb, adjective, adverb, preposition, conjunction, pronoun, interjection.   II

Given selected sentences, recognize simple and complete subjects and predicates.   II

Write sentences in which you use the following grammatical forms. Underline and identify each form that you use.   III
   1. Verb transitive
   2. Verb intransitive
   3. Linking verb
   4. Subject
   5. Direct object
   6. Indirect object
   7. Subject complement
   8. Appositive
   9. Comparative form of an adjective or adverb
  10. Superlative form of an adjective or adverb
  11. At least two prepositional phrases

Recognize adjective clauses, adverb clauses, and noun clauses in written material.   II

Recognize errors in the use of pronouns, adjectives, adverbs, and verbs in written material.   II

Write several sentences that contain prepositional phrases, and underline each prepositional phrase.   III

Write sentences that contain participial phrases, gerund phrases, and infinitive phrases.   III

Write sentences using independent clauses and subordinate (dependent) clauses.   III

Recognize sentence fragments, run-on sentences, relationships between clauses, and parallel structure in written material.   II

01-015-060   Write sentences that are varied and free of ambiguities and that meet generally accepted standards of sentence structure and grammar.   IV

Place all elements of a sentence in logical and meaningful positions.   III

Use pronouns with clear and specific antecedents.   III

Construct sentences from a single viewpoint for maximum clarity   III

Recognize jargon and pretentious language, and state your meaning clearly in appropriate terms.   III

Use words and idiomatic expressions correctly.   III

In a given set of sentences recognize clichés and redundancies, and rewrite the sentences to avoid them.   III

Organize sentences for pertinent ideas, emphasis of point, and smooth relation of relevant details.   IV

Write concisely, and structure sentences for the greatest variety and the most effective length.   IV

Recognize formal, informal, and nonstandard English and situations where each type is appropriate. II

Write sentences that use standard forms of spelling, capitalization, and punctuation. II

Recognize and apply the principles of English spelling. II

Use punctuation according to standards of written English, and to clarify meaning. III

01-015-065   Write interesting sentences of varied structure that show a coherent sequence of thought. III

Distinguish between dependent and independent clauses. I

Identify comma splices and other run-on sentences, and connect independent clauses appropriately. I

Recognize and use parallel structure appropriately. III

Achieve sentence variety by using simple, compound, complex, and compound-complex forms and by varying sentence beginnings. III

01-015-070   Write sentences that demonstrate your knowledge of the fundamental rules of grammar. III

Given a personal pronoun and a verb form, combine them to make a contraction. II

Given a sentence containing noun phrases and clauses, recognize the function of each phrase or clause. II

Identify determiners, and tell whether articles are definite or nondefinite. I

Tell whether the verb phrase in a given sentence contains a form of *be* or another verb. I

Given a form of *be* in a sentence, recognize the structure that follows as a noun phrase, an adjective, or an adverbial of place. II

Given a list of simple sentences containing adverbials, describe each adverbial as an adverbial of place, of manner, or of time. II

Distinguish between transitive and intransitive verbs. III

Given a group of sentences containing verbals, identify the verb in the verbal as transitive or intransitive. If it is transitive, name its object. I

01-015-075 **Using the principles of transformational grammar, change sentence form and meaning through use of single words, phrases, and clauses. III**

Given a list of noun phrases, list the possessive form for each phrase. I

Transform a sentence into a noun phrase by putting the adjective between the determiner and the noun of the subject. III

Make a complex sentence out of a pair of simple sentences. III

Recognize the eight reflexive pronouns, and use them in sentences. II

Make an affirmative sentence negative. III

Given the modals *have, be,* and *do,* use each with the word *not,* rewriting the pairs of words as contractions. II

Transform a statement into a question. III

Rewrite as a *where* question a sentence that has an adverbial of place in the predicate. II

Rewrite as a *when* question a sentence that has an adverbial of time in the predicate. II

Rewrite as a *how* question a sentence that has an adverbial of manner in the predicate. II

Rewrite as a *whom* or a *what* question a sentence that has an object of a verb in the predicate. II

Rewrite a sentence as a question by replacing the subject with *who* or *what*. II

Given a basic sentence containing a transitive verb, write the sentence in passive form. III

Given a sentence containing a dangling modifier, rewrite it, making the sentence grammatical by changing the matrix from passive to active or from active to passive. II

Use transformational grammar to combine several single sentences into one sentence or to break up sentences into shorter ones. III

Rewrite two simple sentences as a third sentence by changing one of the simple sentences into a relative clause. II

Rewrite two simple sentences as a third sentence by compounding, using the conjunctions *and, or,* and *but.* II

Given a group of sentences containing relative clauses, classify them as restrictive or nonrestrictive clauses. II

01-015-080   **Use various types of sentence structure, and explain the purposes of such varieties. III**

Given a declarative sentence (statement), recognize the complete subject and the complete predicate. II

In a question or an inverted declarative sentence, recognize the complete subject and complete predicate and the simple subject and simple predicate. II

Write sentences using the noun–verb (N–V) sentence pattern. III

Write sentences using the noun–verb–noun (N–V–N) sentence pattern. III

Write at least five sentences using the noun–linking verb–noun (N–LV–N) sentence pattern. III

Write sentences using the noun–linking verb–adjective (N–LV–ADJ) sentence pattern. III

Write sentences using compound subjects or compound predicates, or both. III

Rewrite two simple sentences as one compound sentence. II

Given an affirmative statement, transform it to a negative statement, an affirmative question, or a negative question. III

Classify a given sentence as one of the four types of sentences: declarative, exclamatory, imperative, interrogative. II

Punctuate sentences in order to write compound sentences and eliminate run-on sentences. III

Writing Skills

01-020-005   **Write paragraphs that show unity of idea and appropriate organization of introductory, supporting, and concluding sentences.**   III

Define *paragraph,* and name the characteristics of a well-constructed paragraph.   I

State the function of a topic sentence.   I

Write a paragraph that develops a central idea without repetition and without straying from the topic.   III

Write a paragraph in which all the ideas are smoothly related to each other.   III

01-020-010   **Write paragraphs that show unity of idea and logical development.**   IV

Describe what is essential in writing sentences that are free of ambiguities.   II

Recognize the basis of inductive and deductive reasoning.   II

Make valid generalizations, and recognize those that are not valid.   III

Classify terms and ideas to determine their interrelationships, and recognize when ideas are improperly related.   II

Draw valid conclusions from properly related statements or premises, and recognize conclusions incorrectly drawn from the argument on which they are based.   III

Identify the underlying assumptions on which an argument is based, whether or not they are stated, to determine whether the reasoning is sound.   II

Recognize assumptions that are false, based on insufficient evidence, or contain undefined terms.   II

Identify illogical cause-and-effect reasoning and arguments based on irrelevant issues, emotional appeal, exaggeration, and false analogy. I

Distinguish between valid evidence and false evidence, and recognize when an inference drawn from evidence is reasonable. II

Given examples of the following logical fallacies, identify the specific fallacies and rewrite the examples to make them logically correct. III
1. Undefined or abstract terms
2. Overgeneralization
3. *Post hoc, ergo propter hoc* ("after this, therefore because of this")
4. False analogies
5. *Non sequitur* (conclusion does not follow from evidence)
6. *Ignoratio elenchi* (arguing off the point)
7. Sampling (insufficient evidence)

01-020-015 **Use various forms and techniques to demonstrate skill in expository writing. III**

From a list of topics, recognize the topic that would be most suitable for development in a paragraph of about 150 words. II

Write a topic sentence suitable for development in a paragraph of about 150 words. The sentence should be a generalization, and it should be logical. III

Write three paragraphs, using expressions that link sentences by signaling relationships between them, and underline the transitional expressions. III

Write a paragraph using details to develop the topic sentence. III

Write a paragraph using comparisons to develop the topic sentence. III

Use facts and opinions to develop the topic sentence of a paragraph. III

From a topic sentence, write a paragraph that presents a cause-and-effect relationship. III

Write a closing sentence for a paragraph that strengthens and unifies the main impression of the paragraph and makes the reader feel that it is complete. III

01-020-020 Combine concepts, principles, and generalizations by organizing sentences and paragraphs to develop a topic. V

Given groups of words, classify each group as a sentence or a phrase, and add words to each phrase to make it a sentence. II

Write a paragraph, observing the following guide-lines. III
1. Select a topic sentence.
2. Write about one idea.
3. Develop sentences in sequence.

Write an organized explanation of a process. III

Organize paragraphs in an essay to support a central idea. IV

Write an introduction that presents and limits the topic, a body that develops it, and a concluding paragraph. V

Write a short essay that supports your opinion on a given subject, or present a short speech that supports your side in an argument on a given subject. IV

Write a critical review, analyzing a television program or movie with which you are familiar. IV

After drawing a diagram that shows the working parts of an original invention, prepare complete and sequential directions for operation of the invention. III

Conduct an interview with a classmate, and write a report of your interview. III

From an outline that you have prepared and with notes you have collected, write a report according to given specifications. III

Write an article for a school newspaper, using criteria of effective journalism. V

Given a list of references to books, magazines, personal interviews, and encyclopedias, put the references in correct bibliographic order and form. II

Suggest a topic for a report that informs, entertains, or presents an argument. II

01-020-025 **Write a personal essay that makes a point clearly and effectively without unnecessary words or irrelevant ideas. V**

Write coherent paragraphs by using patterns of definition, description, comparison and contrast, and words that are specific and concrete. IV

Determine what kind of answer is called for by an essay question. IV

Express ideas clearly and concisely in a personal essay. V

Define a thing, an idea, or a process either simply or at length. I

Recognize the connotative meanings of words, and use them to intensify and enrich language. II

01-020-030 **Prepare a written report that presents ideas in logical form and sequence. V**

Write an outline for a given selection to show main ideas and supporting details. III

Given two or more paragraphs, write a topic outline in the correct form, using one level of indentation. III

After reading a selection of prose, summarize the main points in the selection. III

After reading a given literary selection in a specific category, write a review based on your personal reaction to the selection. III

Select data from library sources, and write a research paper according to specifications.   V

Summarize an author's ideas, analyze them logically, and evaluate them in a personal essay.   V

Write a paper based on the definition of an idea, an object, or an event.   III

Write your definition of success in an essay that includes an introduction, a body, and a conclusion. The essay should also contain examples of persons who measure up to your definition.   III

Given an article and its summary, recognize whether the summary is a précis.   II

Use the various elements of précis writing by reading a given literary selection and writing a short précis of it.   III

After examining given factual material represented graphically, write a one-paragraph factual report to summarize the significant facts that this material presents.   II

Paraphrase a poem or literary passage.   II

01-020-035   Write an essay that demonstrates your ability to select specific and vivid words, write concise and vigorous sentences, and combine sentence patterns effectively for texture and interest.   V

Match predicate verbs with their subjects and complements, and form and use verb tenses appropriately throughout an essay.   I

Recognize basic sentence elements, arrange them in a properly structured sentence, and subordinate and relate them in a variety of ways in an essay.   II

Differentiate modifiers according to their functions, and relate them to the elements they modify in an essay you have written.   III

Apply generally accepted rules of spelling, punctuation, and capitalization to writing standard English. III

Select a level of language appropriate to your purpose, and write an essay that communicates your meaning clearly, simply, and directly. III

Write an essay using paragraphs that have unity and coherence, organizing ideas clearly and logically to support a central idea. III

Describe how you would add interest and impact to your writing. III

01-020-040 **Given a specific point of view from which to classify people or things, develop a scheme of classification that fulfills these requirements. V**
1. There is only one principle applied at each stage of the classification.
2. The subclassifications under each classification account for all the members in the classification.

Write a paper that gives information about people or things according to a scheme of classification determined by a specific point of view. III

Given a class of people or things, recognize specific individuals or things in that class. II

Identify three ways in which one person or thing can be compared with another person or thing. I

Write a paper in which you compare one person or thing with another person or thing. Before you begin your comparison, state the particular way in which you will make your comparison and the pattern of organization you will use to make your comparison. V

Given something to be analyzed, describe three ways in which it may be analyzed. II

In a written technical description, present a complete and systematic body of information about a given object for sale. III

Given the name of a particular organization or process, analyze in a paper the manner in which the parts of the organization or process work together. IV

Recall something said or written that brought about a definite change in your behavior. Write a brief narrative of what happened to make you change, including the circumstances of your life at the time of the change, what it was that was said or written, who said or wrote it, and what the change in your behavior was. III

01-020-045 Using the criteria of logic, systematically develop a written presentation in support of or against a specific view. V

Write an essay that presents contrasting viewpoints, including the following features. V
1. Identify authors and sources (if you choose to write about viewpoints in published material).
2. Present points of view accurately.
3. Use specific detail from your sources.
4. Explain the logic of arguments in favor of one point of view.
5. Observe the criteria for organization.

Develop a written argument on the affirmative or the negative side of a current issue, emphasizing techniques of effective persuasion. V

01-020-050 Show that you can summarize an article or a book, make generalizations about the ideas involved, and describe the author's conclusions. IV

Given a paragraph and a list of generalizations about the paragraph, recognize the generalizations that are true. II

Given a magazine article or other similar source, summarize it briefly. II

Apply the skill of sequencing to organize material for an oral presentation. III

Form several generalizations about a book of your choice. IV

Examine given factual material represented graphically, and write a one-paragraph factual report to summarize the significant facts that this material presents. III

01-020-055 **Analyze a sample of your writing and the process you went through in writing it, and use your analysis as a guide to assess whether or not you have developed the writing skills you need to survive in college. VI**

Describe techniques for handling information efficiently and effectively, and select writing samples that demonstrate this skill. III

Describe the differences between academic writing and informal writing, quoting from samples of your own work. II

Prepare written material according to exact specifications. III

Write paragraphs that show unity of idea and logical organization of introductory, supporting, and concluding sentences. III

Write sentences that meet generally accepted standards of sentence structure and grammar, and use standard forms of spelling, capitalization, and punctuation. III

Select an appropriate topic for a paper. II

Locate, gather, and organize relevant, up-to-date information for use in a report or thesis. III

Evaluate your ability to work independently, basing your judgment on your preparation of a research paper and using the following criteria. VI
1. Did you set up and meet deadlines for completing elements of the task?
2. Did you get approval of various steps as required?
3. Did you go to appropriate sources for assistance when needed?
4. Did the final paper meet format requirements exactly?
5. Was the final paper completed on time without last-minute confusion?

Document information in a report or thesis, using footnotes and bibliography in standard format.   III

Develop an idea effectively in a paper, writing a logically structured outline and following it.   IV

01-020-060   Use a variety of techniques in writing for different purposes.   III

Given a list of descriptive words and phrases, explain which would be effective in expressing specific emotions.   II

Given two passages that describe a tragic event, recognize the passage that understates the event.   II

Write a descriptive passage about a tragic event, using understatement.   III

Given two passages that describe a situation of conflict, recognize the passage that shows you the situation rather than tells you about it.   II

Write several passages that describe situations of conflict.   III

Use two words to sum up conflicting natures of an object or idea in a compressed conflict, and then write a short paragraph justifying the meaning of your compressed conflict. For example, a compressed conflict describing a fire might be "life-saving destroyer."   III

Recognize style differences in written material.   II

Given two sentences that describe the same person, recognize the sentence that focuses your attention on the person described rather than on the person who wrote the sentence.   II

Write a description of a person, using nouns and verbs that show the person described rather than merely tell about the person.   III

Given two passages that describe the same location, recognize the passage that contains nouns and verbs that show the reader the location rather than merely tell the reader about it.   II

Describe a person who communicates effectively.   III

Write two extended metaphors of approximately 100 words, one interpreting the experience of winning and the other interpreting the experience of losing.   III

Write a description for each of two characters who react differently to failure: one who is strengthened by failure, and one who is weakened by failure.   III

Write a descriptive passage about a location, a person, or an event in which the specific tone you give to the passage clearly indicates your attitude toward your subject.   III

Given a passage that has a specific tone, identify what the tone of the passage tells about the author's attitude toward the subject.   I

Use dialog to develop characterization.   III

Write a two-page dialog between two persons who hold opposing views.   III

Write a dialog that shows four or more of the following things about each person in the dialog: age, sex, occupation, interests, temperament, outlook.   III

Create a mood of expectancy in a description through appropriate choice of words and appropriate length of sentences.   III

Identify at least three ways in which one person or thing can be compared with another person or thing.   I

Given something to be analyzed, describe several ways in which it may be analyzed.   III

Given one or more figures of speech that interpret a particular human experience, identify the experience interpreted.   I

Given a particular human experience, write an extended metaphor of about 150 words to interpret that experience.   III

Given several ironic statements in their context, classify them as lighthearted, fun-poking irony; serious, thought-provoking irony; bitter sarcasm.   II

Write three ironic statements that illustrate each of the following degrees of irony: fun-poking, thought-provoking, and sarcasm. Your statements should be a minimum of 50 words long. There is no maximum.   III

01-020-065   Using the techniques of creative writing, combine concepts, principles, and generalizations by writing original compositions.   V

Relate two different things, such as a doorbell and a rattlesnake, by writing a paragraph in which you make connections between ideas.   V

Write a paragraph in which you as the author assume the role of a thing, animate or inanimate, that is completely different from your own personal experiences. For instance, see the world from the vantage point of a cloud.   V

After viewing a picture from a magazine or newspaper, write a fictitious newspaper story about what is happening in the picture.   III

Write a descriptive narrative.   V

Write an essay that contains both exposition and argument.   V

Given a written passage that indicates by its tone disapproval of a character's action, rewrite the passage and change the tone so that the same actions are presented favorably (or vice versa).   III

Write a skit or dialog that portrays a comic character from literature, the theatre, television, or your own imagination in an incongruous or humorous setting. (For example, portray Don Quixote in a computer center.)   V

Write a story that shows a young person growing up in a particular location with an increasing awareness of what it means to be an adult in that location.   V

Write a scene of a play, using the techniques of effective drama: soliloquy, aside, dialog and visual clues that set the scene, articulation of scenes (purpose of each scene in relation to the entire play), suspense. Be able to explain how you used each technique.   V

Write an original short story that includes plot, character, point of view, tone, setting, and theme. Be able to explain how you used them in your story.   V

01-020-070   **Prepare various types of outlines.   III**

Given a topic and supporting details, prepare a word or phrase outline in proper form, using one level of indentation.   III

Given a short selection, prepare a proper word or phrase outline of the topic and the supporting details, using one level of indentation.   III

Write an outline for a given selection to show main ideas and supporting details.   III

Given two or more paragraphs, write a topic outline in the correct form, using one level of indentation.   III

Prepare an outline for a report, using notes you have collected from various references.   III

01-020-075   **Combine concepts, principles, and generalizations by producing a factual report from notes and an outline.   V**

Take notes from an oral or written source.   III

Given a list of references to books, magazines, personal interviews, and encyclopedias, put the references in correct bibliographic order and form.   II

Suggest a topic for a report that informs, entertains, or presents an argument.   II

01-020-080   Write a report or thesis according to a specified format, using library reference material.   V

Select an appropriate topic for a report or thesis.   I

After choosing a topic and writing at least five questions about the topic, find appropriate materials to answer the questions.   III

Plan the purpose, central idea, and kinds of writing for a research paper.   III

Locate information in the library through efficient use of the card catalog, periodical guides, and reference books.   III

Given a list of six or more titles of books, locate the titles in the library and recognize them as being fiction or nonfiction.   II

Use the card catalog to research given subject matter, authors, and book titles.   III

Use an encyclopedia to locate topics (using the encyclopedia index and guide words) and specific information (using subheadings and cross references).   III

Find information on specific aspects of a given topic from references.   III

Take notes in a specified form, record all essential bibliographic data, and evaluate the reliability of sources.   III

Write an outline for a report or thesis, with ideas properly grouped and subordinated according to the conventions of outline form.   IV

Write footnote and bibliographical data in the standard forms.   III

01-020-085 Prepare a term paper, consulting a minimum of ten sources; no more than two of these sources may be encyclopedias. Bibliographical information should be given in footnotes. V

Select a topic for research that is of interest to you as a researcher, is researchable from sources available to you, and is sufficiently limited to allow scholarly consideration. I

Write a research paper that meets all of the established rules on form and style. Your paper will include a title page, an introductory statement that explains and limits the topic (a statement of thesis), conclusions drawn as a result of the research, and a complete bibliography. V

01-020-090 Write an essay about a famous person, and include in the paper important facts about that person's public life. In writing your paper, use at least three sources of information—such as books, reference works, and periodicals—and include direct quotations that may be intelligently related within the context of your essay. V

Given the name of a prominent personality, find information about that person in biographical dictionaries. III

Use literary reference books to find the author of a quotation, the literary work in which the quotation appeared, the complete quotation when you know only a part, a few famous lines by any author, and quotations by various authors on a particular subject. III

Show that you can gather and organize relevant, up-to-date information in a report or thesis, and document that information, using footnotes and bibliography in standard format. V

Define the following abbreviations commonly used in footnotes: ibid., loc. cit., op. cit., et al., etc., f. or ff., p. or pp., ed., *sic*, vol(s). I

Recognize the use of a thesaurus to expand your vocabulary. II

01-020-095   Write letters to friends and for business, using the correct format.   III

Identify the formats used for a friendly letter and a business letter, and demonstrate your skill in writing letters of each type.   III

Write a friendly letter that includes the following parts in the correct form: heading, greeting, body, closing, signature.   III

Write a business letter that includes the following parts in the correct form: heading, inside address, formal greeting, body, and closing signature.   III

Review writing friendly letters by writing one to express your ideas, interests, and ideals to a student in another part of the country.   III

Write sample business letters to request information, to express your opinion, to recommend action, and to order something by mail.   III

Identify errors in capitalization, punctuation, and spelling in a given business letter.   I

Using correct format, capitalization, and punctuation, write a business letter of adjustment and address the envelope for the letter.   III

Literature and Literary Criticism

01-025-005   **Show your understanding of genre by classifying literary selections. II**

Define *myth, folktale, legend,* and *fable.* I

Explain the differences between biography and historical fiction. I

Define *short story, novella,* and *novel.* II

Explain the differences between a play and a skit. II

Classify nonfiction selections as belonging to one of the following categories: newspaper or periodical article, essay, biography, autobiography, scientific writing. II

Identify characteristics of each of the following types of poetry: lyric, elegy, sonnet, ode, ballad, dramatic, epic, pastoral, narrative. I

01-025-010   **Select your favorite literary genre, and evaluate your preference based on the particular characteristics of the genre you selected. VI**

Given a piece of writing, classify it as fiction or nonfiction. II

Identify characteristics of each of the following types of prose: novel, short story, drama, biography, autobiography, essay. I

Given several prose stories, recognize examples of a parable and a fable. II

Describe the kinds of love found in novels, short stories, plays, and poems you have read. II

List five characteristics of romanticism in literature, and locate an example of each in your reading. I

Given selections of poetry, differentiate between those expressing sentiment and those expressing sentimentality. III

Prepare and present a short report, oral or written, on the content of a biography. III

Prepare and present a short report, oral or written, on the content of an autobiography. III

01-025-015 **Identify and analyze the similarities and differences between a Greek play, an Elizabethan play, and a modern play. IV**

Tell the story of one of the great heroes of ancient Greece or Rome. I

Identify the origins of drama, tragedy, and comedy. I

Explain the influence of religion on early Greek drama. II

Identify the roles played by the characters in early Greek drama. I

Describe the physical elements of the Greek play. II

List three functions of myths in the ancient world. I

Identify twenty gods or other characters important in Greek mythology, identify each by a brief description, and give the Roman name (if one exists) for each. I

Suggest an example of a myth that explains the origin of some natural phenomenon. II

Given a play, such as *Oedipus Rex,* suggest five reasons why it could be considered a tragedy. II

Given a novel dealing with a modern hero, suggest at least three reasons why it could be considered tragic. II

Explain the influence that politics had on early Elizabethan drama. II

Describe the physical elements of the Elizabethan theater. II

Determine at least three characteristics of *The Tragical History of Doctor Faustus* that make this drama a tragedy. IV

Describe influences that affect modern drama. II

Describe the physical elements of the modern theater. II

01-025-020 Discuss the main and supporting ideas in literary selections. III

Given a short selection with the topic stated, recognize supporting details from a list. II

Summarize the main ideas in each of three selections (one oral, one visual, and one written) that you have chosen. II

Describe the main ideas and supporting details of a book you have read. II

Given a short reading selection, the main idea of the selection, and a list of details, recognize the details that most directly support the main idea. II

Describe the main idea of a book of fiction of your choice. Explain the details that most directly support the main idea. II

Given a list of details about a reading selection that has an obvious conclusion, recognize the details that support the conclusion. II

Recognize several details that support the conclusions you have made from reading a book of your choice. II

From a reading list on a given category, read a short story, an essay, a book, a play, or a poem, and suggest examples of a specific topic developed in that selection. II

In a library find one or two selections related to a specific category. Read the selections and, as you read, recognize passages that illustrate the theme. Include the passages in a journal. II

Given a selection of literature related to a specific category, explain how the selection illustrates that category.   II

After reading a poem, offer your interpretation of the meaning and the poet's intent. Include a description of how form can affect content.   III

Locate articles in the various sections of a newspaper, and answer questions about each of these articles.   I

01-025-025   Show your understanding of literary selections by making inferences based on details.   IV

Given a selection of two or more paragraphs and a list of implied statements, recognize statements about the selection that are valid.   II

In a given passage recognize several facts that are implied but not stated.   II

Given an unfinished selection, predict a future event on the basis of previous events in the selection.   III

After reading up to the last chapter in a book of your choice, predict the outcome.   III

Analyze a given selection by inferring the author's intent and by drawing conclusions from the evidence presented.   IV

Analyze a selection to find the author's hidden meaning by identifying what is implied.   IV

01-025-030   Make judgments regarding the relationships of reading selections to personal experiences.   VI

Compare at least two literary works written about the same subject.   IV

Evaluate the validity of the message in a literary selection in terms of personal experience.   VI

01-025-035   Analyze cause-and-effect relationships in literary selections.   IV

In a given reading selection recognize words and/or phrases that demonstrate cause and those that demonstrate effect.   II

Given a short reading selection, write a brief paragraph explaining cause-and-effect relationships in that selection.   IV

Explain a cause-and-effect relationship in a book of your choice.   II

Discuss ways in which an author of a book of your choice creates causes in order to show characters dealing with subsequent effects.   III

01-025-040   Relate the setting to other components in literary selections.   IV

Given a short reading selection and a list of statements, recognize the statement that best describes the setting.   II

Describe orally or in a paragraph the setting of a book of your choice.   II

Explain the effect of the setting (time in history, place, and particular circumstances of the environment) on the principal characters in a given novel or short story from a specific category.   II

Describe the importance of the setting to an author's style.   II

Discuss the symbolic significance of the setting of a particular work.   III

Compare and contrast the uses of the pastoral setting in classical and eighteenth-century English literature.   IV

Compare and contrast the significance of a rural setting as used by two American novelists.   IV

01-025-045 **Relate plot development to other components in literary selections. IV**

Describe the time, place, characters, and sequence of action in a short story. II

Describe the rising action, climax, and falling action in a given short story. II

Summarize the main conflict in a novel or a short story of your choice in a given category. Include the underlying causes of the conflict and the events that contributed to the conflict, and explain the effect of the final resolution of the conflict on each of the principal characters. III

Define the term *deus ex machina,* and give an example of a plot in which this device is used. III

01-025-050 **Relate the author's intent and/or point of view to plot, setting, and characterization in literary selections. IV**

Given a short story, an essay, a poem, a book, or a play from a specific category, recognize the author's point of view on a topic. II

Given a short story, an essay, a poem, a book, or a play on a specific topic, describe the way in which the author's point of view is developed. II

Given an editorial, recognize the purpose or purposes (explanation, persuasion, criticism, or entertainment) that the editorial serves. II

Discuss a novel in which the story is told through the point of view of one of the characters. III

01-025-055 **Relate mood and tone in literary selections to the author's purpose. IV**

Given a paragraph and a list of phrases describing mood, recognize the phrase that best describes the mood of the paragraph. II

Describe the mood and the particular emotion expressed in a given passage. II

Write a short analysis of the technique used by the author to express an emotion in a selection of prose or poetry. IV

Given two passages on the same topic, recognize the words or phrases that are used to change the tone. II

Analyze the way that meter influences the tone or mood of a poem of your choice. IV

01-025-060 Show your understanding of literary devices in given selections. II

Given a descriptive passage of prose or poetry, recognize similes and metaphors. II

Given a variety of poems, recognize words that demonstrate alliteration. II

Given descriptive words or phrases, pictures, or music, list images brought to mind by each example. I

Recognize examples of personification. II

Given a descriptive paragraph, describe the type of space order used (large-to-small, near-to-far, top-to-bottom, etc.), and recognize the words that show the space order. II

Given a narrative paragraph, explain the time order of the actions. II

Given a passage of poetry, recognize an example of onomatopoeia. II

Recognize examples of "stream of consciousness" writing. II

Recognize examples of allegorical writing. II

01-025-065 **Recognize literary techniques and devices in the short story, the novel, drama, biography, and poetry, and show the relationship of these devices to the author's purpose. IV**

Describe the setting of a short story. II

Recognize examples of repetition in a piece of literature, and explain why repetition is used. II

Recognize examples of foreshadowing in a piece of literature, and explain their use. II

Recognize literary symbols, and explain their symbolic meaning. II

Given one or more figures of speech that interpret a particular human experience, recognize the experience interpreted. II

Given a passage that has a specific tone, explain what the tone of the passage tells about the author's attitude toward the subject. II

Recognize an example of irony, either from your reading or from everyday life, and explain why it is ironic. II

Given several ironic statements in their context, classify them as lighthearted, fun-poking, thought-provoking, or vicious. II

Recognize rhyme scheme by scanning several lines of poetry, and use letter patterns to describe the rhyme scheme. II

Recognize the metric pattern called iambic pentameter. II

Identify the characteristics of a poem written in blank verse and those of a poem written in free verse. I

Recognize the literal and figurative meaning of a symbol. II

Differentiate between the connotative and denotative meanings of words used by poets. IV

01-025-070 **Analyze the major works of an American poet, and give an evaluation of the poet's work. VI**

Write a report about a major American poet, covering various aspects of the poet's life and work. III

Present an oral reading of two poems written by a major American poet. III

Explain the contextual meaning of given excerpts from poems by an American poet. III

Evaluate the relevance of given passages from a poem to your present-day world. VI

Compare the major works of an American poet to the dominant political issues of that poet's time. IV

Trace the theme of the Western frontier in the works of a nineteenth-century American poet. II

Select a modern poet, and relate recurring themes of that poet's work to contemporary life and events. IV

01-025-075 **Demonstrate your understanding and ability to evaluate the major works of British poets. VI**

Relate the establishment of the Anglican Church by Henry VIII to the works of major poets of the time. III

Give three reasons for the flourishing of drama in England in the seventeenth century. III

Identify examples of Georgian poetry, and evaluate its significance in the transition of poetic style from the nineteenth to the twentieth century. I

Match three romantic poets with examples of their poetry. I

Identify examples of Scottish vernacular poetry. I

Write a five-page essay on the changing images of women in British poetry written by men from the seventeenth to the twentieth century. V

Trace the theme of empire in the works of a major British poet. II

01-025-080 **Evaluate nineteenth-century naturalism and twentieth-century realism, and compare these styles in two prominent novels from each period. VI**

Describe the ways in which the novel in the ninteenth century reflected on the human condition. II

Explain why *naturalism* was a term applied to the literary mode of this period. II

Analyze the image of women in the works of a nineteenth-century male author, and compare it to the image of women in the works of a female author of the same period. IV

Evaluate the influence of expatriation on a twentieth-century American novelist. VI

Identify examples of "stream of consciousness" writing and at least one twentieth-century novelist who used the technique. I

01-025-085 **Evaluate the relationship of literary contributions of black writers to development of an understanding of the historical and contemporary problems of black Americans. VI**

Recognize two or three distinct evolutionary stages in a black writer's life, and give at least one example of how this awareness or insight is reflected in the author's works. II

Recognize at least three examples from the *Autobiography of Malcolm X* that illustrate why Malcolm X felt blacks have been robbed of their identity in America. II

Describe James Baldwin's account of his childhood experiences and those of an individual from a different minority group living in America, listing similarities and differences in their childhood experiences. II

Write a paper or produce a tape, developing an incident or a quotation from the literary work of a black author that you find particularly relevant to you or to your place in society.   V

In a two-page essay compare and contrast the ideas of Martin Luther King, Jr., and Malcolm X on the best hope for black–white relations in American society.   V

Describe the black American's problem of double identity, and explain how at least one black writer has dealt with it.   II

Find five examples from poetry or prose by black writers that clearly negate a stereotyped concept of blacks.   III

In poems by black writers, recognize at least three universal themes dealt with that are common to human experience (such as love, grief, and search for self) and describe how the poet individualizes the theme.   III

From literature and from other forms of artistic expression (art, music, etc.), find and describe examples that illustrate at least five distinctive aspects of black culture.   II

From your reading and from other observations (photos, television, films, records), suggest at least four specific examples of how blacks have used the weapons of humor or creativity against racialism and indifference.   II

01-025-090   **Demonstrate your ability to understand and evaluate the techniques that Shakespeare employed in comedy and tragedy, and then distinguish the major characteristics of both types of drama.   VI**

Summarize the plot of one of Shakespeare's dramas.   II

Describe four important personality traits of each of the main characters in a Shakespearean drama and explain, by referring to the text of the play, why you believe that the characters have these traits.   II

Recognize six characteristics of Shakespearean tragedy in a play of your choice, and find a specific example of each.   I

Analyze one of the principal problems presented in a Shakespearean drama. These may include the problems of loyalty, communication, governmental power, insurrection, idealism, martyrdom, or ambition.   IV

List six characteristics of Shakespearean comedy found in a play of your choice, and give a specific example of each.   I

Describe a Shakespearean tragic hero and a Greek tragic hero, citing at least three similarities and three differences.   II

01-025-092   **Write a scene of your own by using the following techniques of effective drama, and explain how you used each technique: soliloquy, aside, dialog and visual clues that set the scene, articulation of scenes (purpose of each scene in relation to the entire play), suspense.   V**

From your observations and reading, cite three or four examples that show how comedy very often borders on tragedy.   III

Discuss the differences between comedy and tragedy, and describe how Shakespeare elicited appropriate emotional response from his audience.   III

Find historical information about the life of a character who is important in one of Shakespeare's plays (e.g., Hamlet, Macbeth, King Henry V, Julius Caesar).   II

Find information about Elizabethan drama in general and the Globe Theatre in particular, and relate this information to your understanding of a play by Shakespeare.   IV

Compare and contrast the uses of low-life characters in a comedy and in a tragedy by Shakespeare.   IV

In a play of your choice, select at least three separate speeches by a major character, and demonstrate the character's development in the course of the play by analyzing changes in tone and imagery in the selected speeches. IV

Compare and contrast the attitudes of a character in a tragedy and a character in a comedy to a specific subject such as love, the social hierarchy, or obedience to parents or rulers. Use quotations to support your ideas. IV

Analyze the significance of the names of three characters in a play or plays of your choice. IV

Discuss the significance of a "play within a play" in a Shakespearean drama of your choice. III

01-025-095 **Investigate changes that have occurred in the development of English, and develop a hypothesis related to contemporary changes in language. V**

Given a list of twenty adjectives and nouns pertaining to a single area, explain the etymology of the words, explain how each is used today, and suggest how each might be used in the future. II

Given a list of fifteen words pertaining to the area of mood and feeling, explain the etymology of each word and give examples of its use today. II

Using references, represent chronologically the following events and influences that affected the English language. III
1. Modern English becomes the common tongue.
2. Germanic tribes invade England (*Beowulf* written, place and date unknown).
3. In Medieval England the Church becomes a major influence on language.
4. Norman French is the language of court and school.
5. Chaucer writes in English (Middle English).
6. Printing is invented in Belgium.
7. Caxton's Flemish workers influence English.
8. Renaissance humanism influences English.
9. The British Empire expands and the English language changes (as in America).

Using references, represent on a time scale the following invasions that effected changes in the English language: Picts, Danes, Normans, Anglo-Saxons and Jutes, and Romans. III

Describe, with specific examples, changes in the English language that indicate its popularization (the language of written English approximating the language and style of spoken English). II

Write a small dictionary of dialect and slang, presenting entries in alphabetical order. Include several examples, labeled dialect, slang, jargon, argot, and cant; a clear definition for each entry (avoid using the root of the word to define the entry, such as *groovy*, "the state of being in the groove"); a context following each definition that shows how the word is being used; a listing in the front of the dictionary that defines the meaning of your labels (dialect, slang, jargon, argot, and cant); and a parts-of-speech label for each entry. V

Find and list British English terms and phrases equivalent to the following American English ones, checking for differences in spelling, vocabulary, and pronunciation. III

1. humor	8. grade crossing	15. medieval
2. traveler	9. ax	16. movies
3. gas	10. windshield	17. check (credit)
4. theater	11. hood (of car)	18. check (baggage)
5. freight train	12. catalog	19. castle
6. truck	13. wrench	20. charm
7. wagon	14. streetcar	

Develop a research paper on a limited aspect of the topic "Place Names in the United States." Consider using the names of states, counties, cities, towns, villages, or streets. Consider such influences as word origin, spelling and changes in spelling, pronunciation and changes in pronunciation, meanings, and exceptions to general trends in any of these areas. V

01-025-100 **Perceive relationships in theories of language development. IV**

Match each of these terms from the major areas of linguistic specialization with a statement that describes it accurately: *dialect study, grammar, descriptive linguistics, language history, usage, lexicography, semantics, psycholinguistics.* I

Describe three major theories about the origin of language, select the theory you favor, and explain your opinion. II

After examining both sides of the controversy, explain whether you think it is the lexicographer's responsibility to *prescribe* language or to *describe* language. Give four supportive reasons for your conclusion, citing at least three sources. II

Apply to examples from current speech and writing the idea that individuals may be judged by their language. III

01-025-105 **Use techniques of literary criticism to evaluate components and relationships in short stories. VI**

Recognize the theme (or main idea) of a short story, and relate it to a situation with which you are familiar. II

Given a short story to read, describe its setting and explain why the setting is important to the story. II

Given a short story and statements about the story, recognize the statement that best describes its conflict and the one that best describes its climax. II

Analyze a short story to determine the point of view from which it is told. IV

Analyze a short story to determine the author's attitude toward the main character. IV

Analyze three ideas you received from reading a short story. Indicate which idea you think is the most important and which idea you think the author considers the most important. IV

Given a list of possible story plots, suggest possibilities for their development. II

Given a list of possible story plots and a list of several characters, suggest the characters who might be appropriately included in the development of the plot. II

Write an original short story that includes all of the major components (plot, character, point of view, tone, setting, and theme), and be able to explain how you used them in your story. V

Given a short story, determine the author's attitude toward the subject, characters, and situation in the story. Identify the clues that led to your conclusion. IV

01-025-110 **Use techniques of literary criticism and interpretation to evaluate components and relationships in novels. VI**

After reading a novel, summarize the important incidents in the plot and recognize the climax. II

Describe the following elements of a given novel: plot, setting, point of view, characterization. II

Discuss a life situation described in a novel from the point of view of credibility. III

Discuss the central theme in a novel, considering how the novel illustrates it and how the author might apply it to a contemporary situation. III

Determine the setting of a novel and its effect on the characters and the plot. IV

In a novel list examples of foreshadowing. II

Analyze the symbolism of a novel, and interpret examples. IV

Write a paper explaining how the main events in a book support the theme, and give examples of the author's main technique for building the climax (i.e., suspense, action, character analysis, conflict). II

Explain how an author uses techniques of short-story writing to create an effective novel. II

Analyze the importance of the arrangement of events in a novel by listing the events in the order in which the author placed them and then rearranging the order of those you consider key scenes. Evaluate the effect of the rearrangement on the novel as a whole, on the characters and their development, and on the reader. IV

After listing the main incidents in a novel, select one and write an alternate incident that the author might have chosen to illustrate a point. Evaluate the effectiveness of the change on the novel as a whole. VI

Write a different ending for the novel you have chosen, keeping in mind the nature of the characters involved and the pattern of events leading to the ending. Evaluate the effects of both the author's ending and yours. VI

Classify three criticisms by nineteenth-century social novelists as economic, political, or social criticism. II

Evaluate the influence of cinematic techniques on a current novel, using examples to substantiate your opinion. VI

01-025-115 Discuss the concepts of credibility and/or absurdity with respect to science fiction. III

Given a work of science fiction you have read that deals with techniques of mind control, recognize the techniques that influence the behavior of the main character. II

Given two works of science fiction—one that pictures the future world as a Utopia and the other that gives an opposite impression—discuss how each deals with freedom of the individual, the family unit, education, government, work, and leisure time. III

Write a dictionary of vocabulary terms specific to a science-fiction novel such as *Out of the Silent Planet* or *Dune.* III

Summarize the main events of a science-fiction story you have read. II

Interpret allusions made in the course of a science-fiction story or novel. II

Discuss a philosophical or ethical point raised in a science-fiction story or novel. III

Discuss examples of science fiction that anticipated current scientific knowledge or technology and examples of scientific discoveries that spawned new works of science fiction. III

01-025-120 **Describe the relationships of character to motivation and action, and make judgments regarding the author's effectiveness in showing these relationships. VI**

Describe orally or in writing the physical appearance and personality of the three most important characters in a specific novel. II

Given a list of words that describe personality characteristics, match these with characters from some stories you have read. I

Given a list of specific characters from your reading, match them with a list of possible descriptions of these characters. I

Describe the characteristics and motives of characters in a short story. II

Describe the main character of a short story, and tell which traits the author emphasizes. Give three examples from the story that show different ways of revealing character. II

Analyze the similarities between the thoughts and feelings of the main character in a short story and those of someone you know. (This "someone" may be you.) IV

Write a paragraph describing an action for each of the following types of characters from short stories, novels, and plays you have read: two characters whose actions are entirely responsible, two whose actions are responsible in some respects, and two whose actions are entirely irresponsible. Explain why your examples are valid. III

Analyze a play or novel with a comic hero (such as *Man of La Mancha* with Don Quixote or *Henry IV*, Part I, with Falstaff) to locate examples that show both comic and philosophic insights about human nature. IV

After reading a play or novel with a comic hero, recognize by name and example at least four of the devices the author uses to produce a comic effect. II

Given a list of literary works about heroic adventures, recognize the obstacles the hero must face and the specific qualities of heroism revealed in meeting each obstacle. II

Given a character of heroic proportions, evaluate whether or not the character is realistically presented by the author. Use a given definition of heroic characteristics as your criteria. VI

Analyze the tragedies surrounding three contemporary world figures whose careers have had a tragic end. Cite examples of how poor judgment and/or qualities in each individual's character were related to the tragedy. IV

01-025-125 **Given a character from a novel, a short story, or a play that you have read, decide whether a decision made by the character is ethically wrong or ethically right, and describe the consequences of that decision. VI**

Given a decision made by a character from a short story, a play, or a novel that you have read, recognize from the following list the way the character made the decision: independently, through the influence of another person, through circumstance, or through two or more of these influences. Explain whether this way is consistent with what is known about the character. II

Given decisions of main characters in Puritan literature that you have read, recognize the elements of Puritanism in their decisions. II

Write a two-paragraph description for each of two characters who react differently to failure: one who is strengthened by failure and one who is weakened by failure. III

Given characters from novels, short stories, or plays that you have read, discuss them as follows. II
1. Describe the type of love that exists between two characters.
2. Describe how the love operates.
3. Describe the final consequences for the lover and for the loved.
4. Measure the love against your ideal standards of loving and being loved.

Given characters from novels, short stories, and plays that you have read, analyze the growth and development of love between one individual and another, within the family, and among people in general. IV

Analyze short stories, giving examples of characters who demonstrate the quality of sensitivity or compassion and of characters who communicate an indifference or lack of awareness of others' feelings. State specifically the clues in each case that enabled you to make the differentiation. IV

01-025-130 **From among the works of such contemporary authors as Philip Roth, John Updike, Joyce Carol Oates, Doris Lessing, Kurt Vonnegut, Saul Bellow, Bernard Malamud, Thomas Pynchon, John Barth, Erica Jong, and Joseph Heller, describe a character who exemplifies the following definition of an alienated individual: "An alienated individual is one who feels separated from another individual, a group, or a society." Explain why you regard the character as an alienated individual. V**

Determine the factor(s) in a given novel, short story, or poem that caused a character's alienation. IV

Given alienated characters from novels, short stories, and plays, predict in writing a course their lives might take if they are able to overcome their feelings of alienation. III

Write a paper on one of the following aspects of aliena-tion found in literary works. V
1. Reasons for alienation
2. Consequences of alienation
3. Solutions for the problem of alienation

01-025-135   **Describe the relationships that cause central conflicts between characters and/or ideas, and make judgments on the effectiveness with which the conflicts are pre-sented. VI**

Given two passages that describe a situation of conflict, recognize the passage that shows you the situation rather than tells you about it. II

Explain the difference between internal and external conflict, and give specific examples of each. II

Given situations involving group behavior in which one or more of the following types of conflicts occur, state the probable consequences of the conflict and propose alternate solutions to remove the conflict. Then, after evaluating the plans, decide which plan would provide the most appropriate solution. VI
1. Conflicts about group goals
2. Conflicts about role behavior (differences in role expectations)
3. Conflicts about group norms

Design an original presentation—oral, visual, or written—about any one or a combination of the following: a person in conflict with himself, a person in conflict with another person, a person in conflict with several people, a group in conflict with another group, a nation in conflict with another nation. V

Given examples like the following that involve conflict between mores and laws, recognize reasons for the conflict: prohibition, equal rights for women, and religion and education. II

After watching a television drama involving social conflict, analyze the ways in which social or group pressure affects the behavior of characters in the play.   IV

Given examples of conflict between an individual and the group that person belongs to and a list of characters from stories you have read, predict possible reactions of specific characters to different conflict situations.   III

Given examples of conflict between groups and a list of characters from stories you have read, predict possible reactions of specific characters to different conflict situations.   III

Given a list of ways to solve conflict, select the solutions that might be used effectively in at least three conflicts from your reading.   II

Write a descriptive passage that shows an individual in a situation of conflict.   V

01-025-140   Using techniques of literary criticism, evaluate the effectiveness of a given essay.   VI

After reading an essay, infer the author's purpose (the central idea) and evaluate that author's skill in stimulating a response from the reader. Then analyze your reaction to the ideas expressed in the essay.   VI

After reading an essay, analyze its structure (the means the author uses to achieve purpose), considering these points.   IV
1. What are the main divisions of the essay and their relation to each other?
2. How long and how complex are the paragraphs, and what is their relation to the main point?
3. How formal or informal is the author's language and approach to the reader?

Write an essay describing situations in which you are in a minority and situations in which you are in a majority.   V

Analyze your emotional response to a short story or essay, listing the words, phrases, expressions, and passages that particularly appeal to the reader's senses. Then describe orally the emotional response, such as anger or disgust, that they stirred. IV

01-025-145 **Write an interpretation of an author's ideas in your own words, using the following guidelines: reflect the organizational pattern used by the author, abbreviate accurately the author's ideas, avoid editorial comment, demonstrate clear expression. V**

Delineate an author's theme by identifying the author's position concerning the topic and by referring to ideas within the author's text that support your identification, making comments as needed. IV

Analyze an author's writing, following these criteria. IV
1. Identify and discuss unstated assumptions, fallacies, logical conclusions, rhetorical devices, and consistency in tone.
2. Point out the author's errors in logic and rhetoric without becoming personal or emotional.

Comment on an essay, including the following points. IV
1. Select important ideas from the essay for comment.
2. Distinguish between your ideas and those of the author.
3. Present ideas that support the author's view or offer an alternative view.
4. Use a positive approach.

01-025-150 **Combine concepts, principles, and generalizations to develop your own definition of culture and civilization based on literature that presents an anthropological view of man. V**

Given characters in novels and plays about human society that you have read, determine whether their general behavior is consistent or inconsistent with the following definition of *civilized behavior:* "Civilized behavior is the extent of concern one's actions show for the welfare of other people." In a sentence or two explain the behavior of each character. IV

Given a literary work that deals with people in a particular society, recognize in the makings of that society examples of political elements, economic elements, educational elements, leisure-time or avocational elements, social elements, spiritual or religious elements. For example, a competitive grading system is an educational element in our civilization; the stock market and the graduated income tax are economic elements.   II

Having classified elements in the makeup of a particular society described in novels and plays that you have read, determine those that encourage civilized behavior, those that both encourage and discourage civilized behavior, and those that discourage civilized behavior. As a guide, use the following definition of civilized behavior: "Civilized behavior is the extent of concern a person's actions show for the welfare of other people."   III

Read a literary work about persons of another culture, and describe five of their cultural attitudes, practices, or customs. Then explain why these attitudes, practices, or customs exist, citing the source for your examples.   II

Demonstrate that people of various cultures often express identical emotions. A set of pictures forming a collage, a set of film clips, or a set of audio-tape sequences would be an appropriate demonstration.   III

Describe at least six instances in which practices disapproved of by one culture are acceptable in another culture, and cite your sources.   II

Recognize some attitudes, stereotypes, or biases about people of another cultural, racial, or ethnic group. Be able to cite examples from movies, literature, or personal experience that reinforce or modify the attitude, stereotype, or bias.   II

Discuss the ideas and the mores that formed the background of today's generation of parents. Cite specific examples from all media of the time.   III

Discuss the culture, the philosophy, and the essence of the society that is being created by tomorrow's generation of parents. Cite specific examples of all media from the 1960s.   III

01-025-155 **Analyze the relationship of intellectual and social implications in literature, and evaluate one author's use of this relationship. VI**

Given stories, novels, and plays about young people with a growing awareness of what it means to be an adult, recognize the elements of the adult world of which young people are becoming aware, describe the events that produce this growing awareness, and describe the reactions of young people to their growing awareness. II

Given a list of literary works about young people, suggest examples for each of the following kinds of relationships that exist between characters in the literary works. II
1. An adult helps a young person grow up.
2. An adult helps a young person grow up in some respects and hinders him in others.
3. An adult hinders a young person from growing up.

Based on your observations of conformity in novels, short stories, plays, and life, write an extended definition of the term *conformity*. III

Given novels, short stories, and plays that you have read, recognize areas in which the major character did or did not conform to existing social standards at the time depicted. II

Describe the consequences of the nonconformity of a given literary character who is a nonconformist. II

Analyze poems or songs to locate examples of man's sensitivity or indifference to his fellows or to his environment. IV

Demonstrate man's sensitivity to people and to his environment with cartoons, photographs, or pictures and with newspaper or magazine clippings. III

Discuss social values and evils that cause corruption or make some people victims of their society. III

Recognize definitions of each of the following terms often used in reference to minority groups, and recognize one example of each of these terms: *prejudice, stereotype, discrimination, bigotry, racism, intolerance.* II

Given a list of statements describing group relationships, recognize the statements that show prejudice and those that do not. II

Given a list of prejudicial statements, infer the basis of the author's prejudices in each case: fear, greed, ignorance. II

Given descriptions of particular products that result from applied technology, determine which one of the following categories each product belongs to. Write an essay supporting each classification you make. III
1. Products that may enhance the quality of our lives directly
2. Products that may enhance the quality of our lives indirectly (by freeing us for other pursuits, for example)
3. Products that merely add to the quantity of things heaped up for our use and abuse

Evaluate the extent to which the principal character of a given novel or play that you have read succeeded in achieving the "American dream." (The "American dream" is the belief that any man can raise himself by his bootstraps to become what he wishes to be and to attain what he wishes to have.) VI

Given a selection from a list of literary works dealing with social injustice, recognize attitudes held by characters in those works that either cause or reinforce unjust social conditions. II

From articles, essays, and poems, infer meanings that are given to human freedom by the author. II

Having read a short story, a novel, or a play that deals with the subject of war, describe two attitudes toward war that are revealed by the thoughts, speech, and/or actions of two characters. II

01-025-160   **Write a paper describing the role of the critic; include examples from the work of current critics in your interpretation.   V**

Compare the views of two different critics on the same short story, novel, or play.   IV

Interpret the effect of literary criticism on writing style.   II

Compare the role of the literary critic and the role of the journalist.   IV

Analysis of Mass Media

01-030-005   Combine concepts, principles, and generalizations by producing a simple newspaper (no less than one page) that includes one article of class (local) interest, one article of school (national) interest, one article of community (world) interest, and one article from each of the following sections: classified, sports, theater and entertainment, editorial, comics. V

Find information and employment opportunities in newspapers.

Locate articles in various sections of a newspaper, and answer questions about each of these articles. I

Given a local newspaper, recognize at least one article of local interest, one article of national interest, and one article of world interest. II

Recognize the following parts of a local newspaper: headline page, sports page, classified section, editorials, index. II

Write an article for a school newspaper, using the criteria for effective journalism. V

Write and conduct an interview for a school newspaper, including the interviewed person's name and at least three facts about that person's life. III

Given the lead paragraph from a news story, identify the parts that tell who, what, when, where, and how. I

After reading a selection of poetry involving a historical event, write a newspaper story from the given facts. III

Given a news story and three headlines, recognize the headline that uses the least space in presenting the main fact of the news story. II

Given an editorial, recognize the purpose or purposes (explanation, persuasion, criticism, praise, or entertainment) that the editorial serves.   II

Given a newspaper review of a book, recording, movie, or television show, determine whether or not the review states an opinion, makes a recommendation, includes basic information, or summarizes briefly.   IV

Given examples of classified ads from a newspaper, recognize ads that present all the necessary information.   II

01-030-010   **Describe forms of mass media and analyze the importance of media to individuals and to large populations.   IV**

Describe forms of mass media that can be used to inform, persuade, or entertain a large group of people (such as the population of a country) about a given topic. Explain why each medium is more or less useful for this purpose than the other forms.   II

Describe aspects of mass media that are important economically, and cite examples and effects of media deprivation.   II

Given an example of a particular person's role in society, explain how mass media could help, as well as harm, this person.   II

Explain the difference between commercial and public broadcasting.   II

In written form or in a discussion, support or reject the idea that public broadcasting offers television programs that are more "educational" than those on commercial stations.   IV

01-030-015   Watch ten different TV programs. Evaluate each program, using the following criteria.   VI
1. Was there violence in the program?
2. Was there a social message in the program? What was it?
3. Was there a message of personal value in the program? What was it?
4. Was there evidence of prejudicial attitudes in the program? What was the situation?
5. Did the program contribute to your intellectual growth?
6. Was the program primarily an escape from reality?

Suggest ways that TV can affect a person's family life and education.   II

Explain why violence is often included in television news, movies, and series, including those with detective, spy, western, war, horror, and science-fiction formats.   II

Using the mass media as resources, suggest reasons for two or more viewpoints on a controversial social issue.   II

Describe three advantages of listening to different, conflicting points of view.   II

01-030-020   Make judgments about media by evaluating different presentations.   VI

After viewing selected photographs and/or listening to records or tapes of dramatic scenes, analyze any reactions you experienced by listing ideas or sensations that led to your response.   IV

Given a particular event, determine some of the causes and effects of the event and express your findings in a paper.   IV

Demonstrate how people display opposite emotions about the same event with at least three examples from pictures in newspapers or magazines.   III

In writing and/or discussion, analyze both written and oral presentations to locate faulty generalizations.   IV

Given a reading selection containing a theme supported by facts, determine the accuracy of supporting details by consulting appropriate special references. III

Analyze a news story as reported in two different publications, broadcasts, or telecasts to locate examples of bias or misleading use of facts revealed by the way the various news media dealt with the same story. IV

Analyze a statement made for the mass media to determine the author's attitude toward minority groups and equal opportunity. IV

After watching a TV drama involving social conflict, determine how social or group pressure affects the behavior of characters in the play. IV

After viewing four or five TV programs for two or three weeks, evaluate them by producing a TV guide that indicates the nature of each program, the audience for whom it is intended, and your critique of the program. VI

Summarize ways in which the consumer can avoid signing fraudulent contracts and can prevent himself from being legally bound to exorbitant, long-term financial agreements. II

Analyze a personal reaction to a movie involving a strong bond of sympathy for one of the major characters. Label the strongest emotion you felt as you identified with the character, and analyze the technique used by the director to obtain that reaction from you. IV

Suggest films that are appropriate for showing to high-school students in a film-study course, and explain your choice of films. II

In a working group, produce a brief film of one of the following. V
1. A commercial or a parody of a commercial
2. A documentary on a current topic
3. An art film
4. A narrative film with a serious theme

01-030-025   Use the techniques of mass media for persuading an audience. V

Given examples of common propaganda devices, classify them as being associated with name-calling, glittering generalities, transfer, testimonial, plain folks, card-stacking, and bandwagon. II

Given examples of common propaganda appeals, classify them as being associated with survival, safety, belonging, prestige, or fulfillment. II

Given the name and a brief description of a past propaganda campaign, find additional information about the campaign so that you can describe one direct consequence of the campaign and two indirect consequences of the campaign. You must support the validity of the direct consequence you list by identifying the source of your information. Furthermore, you must list at least two different sources of information. III

Develop a propaganda campaign for or against an idea or action, making use of at least one of the common propaganda devices and at least one of the common propaganda appeals. V

Discuss the possibility that social values in America are controlled or at least manipulated by TV producers and advertisers, and cite examples to illustrate your points. III

Recognize ploys and devices used by automobile salesmen in selling automobiles. II

With examples from newspapers and magazines, illustrate the techniques used by advertisers to create favorable attitudes toward their product and to persuade customers to buy. II

Explain each of the following techniques used by film makers, and relate each to the process of communication: framing, long long-shot, long-shot, medium shot, close close-up, close-up, motion, camera position (angle), facial features, background, contrasts, editing, montage, lighting, color, music, sound effects, commentary, dialog. II

01-030-030   **Describe the techniques of advertising and analyze its effects. IV**

Given a list of guidelines for producing advertisements, recognize which guidelines apply to television commercials, magazine ads, billboards, and radio commercials. II

From a television, radio, billboard, or magazine advertisement, differentiate between information that is implied and information that is stated. III

From a television, radio, billboard, or magazine advertisement, recognize information that is misleading and explain why it is misleading. II

In a report (written or verbal), investigate the prospect of a "no advertising" policy (or a minimum-advertising policy) on TV and radio. Explain what you believe the effects would be—on the medium and on the economy—and offer evidence to support your conclusions. IV

Analyze the support provided to public television, and determine whether or not this kind of support may become a form of advertising. IV

Appendix

Listening and Speaking

01-005-005   Given short listening passages, recall details and the order of their presentation.   I

01-005-010   Given short listening passages, recognize and recall relationships and unifying elements.   II

01-005-015   Given short listening passages, recognize and recall sequence and patterns.   II

01-005-020   In a situation dependent on following oral directions, perform as the directions specify.   III

01-005-025   Understand and apply the skills necessary to building listening comprehension, and demonstrate comprehension by taking accurate notes.   III

01-005-030   Apply a variety of techniques to improve your understanding of oral directions.   III

01-005-035   In oral passages of several paragraphs, recognize subdivisions of the main idea and their sequence and arrangement.   II

01-005-040   Recognize the organization of a given oral passage.   II

01-005-045   Relate speaker's point of view to content in a talk.   IV

01-005-050   Given oral passages of several paragraphs, recognize and recall details and main ideas.   II

01-005-055   Given oral passages of several paragraphs, recognize elements of unity and relationships between details and the main idea.   II

01-005-060   Develop criteria for evaluating content and speech techniques, and use these techniques in evaluating oral presentations.   VI

01-005-065   Differentiate between appropriate and inappropriate forms of conversation.   V

01-005-070   Prepare an organized oral report.   III

01-005-075 Present an organized oral report. III

01-005-080 Evaluate the techniques used by a speaker in an oral presentation. VI

01-005-085 Present a speech, using appropriate techniques. III

01-005-090 Produce one of the following forms of nonverbal communication—painting, sculpture, drawing, collage, photograph, movie—to express a feeling, an attitude, or an idea on a specific category. V

01-005-095 Participate in achieving the goals of a discussion group. III

01-005-100 Apply techniques for leading a discussion, and evaluate the result. VI

01-005-105 Participate in group situations in which personal opinions and values are being expressed, and evaluate the outcome of such a situation. VI

01-005-110 Explain the probable source of power in situations where a group or an individual has power over another group or individual. II

01-005-115 Use logic and rhetoric in discussing topics and in presenting oral arguments or debates. V

01-005-120 Discuss the range of expression in an oral presentation. III

01-005-125 Develop dramatic techniques by combining concepts, principles, and generalizations. V

Word Skills

01-010-005   Recognize the importance of auditory discrimination and audiovisual association, and apply these skills in reading and spelling unfamiliar words.   III

01-010-010   Given a chart of graphemic–phonemic relationships, analyze your own misspelled words to determine the patterns of your spelling problems.   IV

01-010-015   Apply skills of phonetic and structural analysis to improve your spelling and reading.   IV

01-010-020   Using a chart of phonetic symbols for reference, translate both oral and written passages into phonetic symbols, and read aloud such passages translated by others.   III

01-010-025   In reading unfamiliar words, apply structural-analysis techniques related to affixes and roots to recognize meaning.   III

01-010-030   Use a dictionary to identify the structure and meaning of words.   III

01-010-035   Use a variety of techniques to infer meanings of unfamiliar words.   III

01-010-040   Explain the meanings of common prefixes, suffixes, and roots derived from other languages, and use this information to infer the meanings of unfamiliar words.   III

01-010-045   Trace the history of a word as a linguistic form.   III

01-010-050   Explain and give examples of regional, ethnic, and dialectical differences in vocabulary, pronunciation, and syntax.   III

01-010-055   Given samples of oral and written language, describe the differences of patterns and make judgments regarding the acceptability of these samples in varied social, educational, and career situations.   VI

01-010-060 Define the term *inflection,* and use inflectional rules as they relate to English. III

01-010-065 Classify words as they function in sentences, distinguishing nouns, verbs, adjectives, and adverbs. II

01-010-070 Analyze the relationship of emotional and psychological impact of words to semantics. IV

Sentence Skills

01-015-005 Write sentences, using the basic parts of speech. III

01-015-010 Use punctuation and capitalization appropriately in writing sentences. III

01-015-015 Recognize and use appropriate internal punctuation in writing sentences. III

01-015-020 Write sentences, using nouns, pronouns, and determiners. III

01-015-025 Write sentences using adjectives and adverbs. Distinguish between single-word adverbs and single-word adjectives. III

01-015-030 Write sentences using verbs and verbals, and identify the relationships of the verbs and verbals to nouns and adverbs in the sentences. III

01-015-035 Differentiate between fragments and kernel sentences, and write examples of each type. III

01-015-040 Differentiate among modifiers according to their functions, and relate them to the elements they modify. III

01-015-045 Distinguish between restrictive and nonrestrictive relative clauses, participles, and appositives. III

01-015-050 Explain agreement in sentences as it relates to pronoun–antecedent agreement and subject–verb agreement. III

01-015-055 Recognize basic grammatical terms and functions, and use them in writing sentences. III

01-015-060 Write sentences that are varied and free of ambiguities and that meet generally accepted standards of sentence structure and grammar. IV

01-015-065 Write interesting sentences of varied structure that show a coherent sequence of thought. III

01-015-070 Write sentences that demonstrate your knowledge of the fundamental rules of grammar. III

01-015-075   Using the principles of transformational grammar, change sentence form and meaning through use of single words, phrases, and clauses.   III

01-015-080   Use various types of sentence structure, and explain the purposes of such varieties.   III

Writing Skills

01-020-005 Write paragraphs that show unity of idea and appropriate organization of introductory, supporting, and concluding sentences. III

01-020-010 Write paragraphs that show unity of idea and logical development. IV

01-020-015 Use various forms and techniques to demonstrate skill in expository writing. III

01-020-020 Combine concepts, principles, and generalizations by organizing sentences and paragraphs to develop a topic. V

01-020-025 Write a personal essay that makes a point clearly and effectively without unnecessary words or irrelevant ideas. V

01-020-030 Prepare a written report that presents ideas in logical form and sequence. V

01-020-035 Write an essay that demonstrates your ability to select specific and vivid words, write concise and vigorous sentences, and combine sentence patterns effectively for texture and interest. V

01-020-040 Given a specific point of view from which to classify people or things, develop a scheme of classification that fulfills these requirements. V
1. There is only one principle applied at each stage of the classification.
2. The subclassifications under each classification account for all the members in the classification.

01-020-045 Using the criteria of logic, systematically develop a written presentation in support of or against a specific view. V

01-020-050 Show that you can summarize an article or a book, make generalizations about the ideas involved, and describe the author's conclusions. IV

01-020-055   Analyze a sample of your writing and the process you went through in writing it, and use your analysis as a guide to assess whether or not you have developed the writing skills you need to survive in college. VI

01-020-060   Use a variety of techniques in writing for different purposes. III

01-020-065   Using the techniques of creative writing, combine concepts, principles, and generalizations by writing original compositions. V

01-020-070   Prepare various types of outlines. III

01-020-075   Combine concepts, principles, and generalizations by producing a factual report from notes and an outline. V

01-020-080   Write a report or thesis according to a specified format, using library reference material. V

01-020-085   Prepare a term paper, consulting a minimum of ten sources; no more than two of these sources may be encyclopedias. Bibliographical information should be given in footnotes. V

01-020-090   Write an essay about a famous person, and include in the paper important facts about that person's public life. In writing your paper, use at least three sources of information—such as books, reference works, and periodicals—and include direct quotations that may be intelligently related within the context of your essay. V

01-020-095   Write letters to friends and for business, using the correct format. III

Literature and Literary Criticism

01-025-005   Show your understanding of genre by classifying literary selections. II

01-025-010   Select your favorite literary genre, and evaluate your preference based on the particular characteristics of the genre you selected. VI

01-025-015   Identify and analyze the similarities and differences between a Greek play, an Elizabethan play, and a modern play. IV

01-025-020   Discuss the main and supporting ideas in literary selections. III

01-025-025   Show your understanding of literary selections by making inferences based on details. IV

01-025-030   Make judgments regarding the relationships of reading selections to personal experiences. VI

01-025-035   Analyze cause-and-effect relationships in literary selections. IV

01-025-040   Relate the setting to other components in literary selections. IV

01-025-045   Relate plot development to other components in literary selections. IV

01-025-050   Relate the author's intent and/or point of view to plot, setting, and characterization in literary selections. IV

01-025-055   Relate mood and tone in literary selections to the author's purpose. IV

01-025-060   Show your understanding of literary devices in given selections. II

01-025-065   Recognize literary techniques and devices in the short story, the novel, drama, biography, and poetry, and show the relationship of these devices to the author's purpose. IV

01-025-070   Analyze the major works of an American poet, and give an evaluation of the poet's work.   VI

01-025-075   Demonstrate your understanding and ability to evaluate the major works of British poets.   VI

01-025-080   Evaluate nineteenth-century naturalism and twentieth-century realism, and compare these styles in two prominent novels from each period.   VI

01-025-085   Evaluate the relationship of literary contributions of black writers to development of an understanding of the historical and contemporary problems of black Americans.   VI

01-025-090   Demonstrate your ability to understand and evaluate the techniques that Shakespeare employed in comedy and tragedy, and then distinguish the major characteristics of both types of drama.   VI

01-025-092   Write a scene of your own by using the following techniques of effective drama, and explain how you used each technique: soliloquy, aside, dialog and visual clues that set the scene, articulation of scenes (purpose of each scene in relation to the entire play), suspense.   V

01-025-095   Investigate changes that have occurred in the development of English, and develop a hypothesis related to contemporary changes in language.   V

01-025-100   Perceive relationships in theories of language development.   IV

01-025-105   Use techniques of literary criticism to evaluate components and relationships in short stories.   VI

01-025-010   Use techniques of literary criticism and interpretation to evaluate components and relationships in novels.   VI

01-025-115   Discuss the concepts of credibility and/or absurdity with respect to science fiction.   III

01-025-120   Describe the relationships of character to motivation and action, and make judgments regarding the author's effectiveness in showing these relationships.   VI

01-025-125 Given a character from a novel, a short story, or a play that you have read, decide whether a decision made by the character is ethically wrong or ethically right, and describe the consequences of that decision. VI

01-025-130 From among the works of such contemporary authors as Philip Roth, John Updike, Joyce Carol Oates, Doris Lessing, Kurt Vonnegut, Saul Bellow, Bernard Malamud, Thomas Pynchon, John Barth, Erica Jong, and Joseph Heller, describe a character who exemplifies the following definition of an alienated individual: "An alienated individual is one who feels separated from another individual, a group, or a society." Explain why you regard the character as an alienated individual. V

01-025-135 Describe the relationships that cause central conflicts between characters and/or ideas, and make judgments on the effectiveness with which the conflicts are presented. VI

01-025-140 Using techniques of literary criticism, evaluate the effectiveness of a given essay. VI

01-025-145 Write an interpretation of an author's ideas in your own words, using the following guidelines: reflect the organizational pattern used by the author, abbreviate accurately the author's ideas, avoid editorial comment, demonstrate clear expression. V

01-025-150 Combine concepts, principles, and generalizations to develop your own definition of culture and civilization based on literature that presents an anthropological view of man. V

01-025-155 Analyze the relationship of intellectual and social implications in literature, and evaluate one author's use of this relationship. VI

01-025-160 Write a paper describing the role of the critic; include examples from the work of current critics in your interpretation. V

Analysis of Mass Media

01-030-005   Combine concepts, principles, and generalizations by producing a simple newspaper (no less than one page) that includes one article of class (local) interest, one article of school (national) interest, one article of community (world) interest, and one article from each of the following sections: classified, sports, theater and entertainment, editorial, comics. V

01-030-010   Describe forms of mass media and analyze the importance of media to individuals and to large populations. IV

01-030-015   Watch ten different TV programs. Evaluate each program, using the following criteria. VI
1. Was there violence in the program?
2. Was there a social message in the program? What was it?
3. Was there a message of personal value in the program? What was it?
4. Was there evidence of prejudicial attitudes in the program? What was the situation?
5. Did the program contribute to your intellectual growth?
6. Was the program primarily an escape from reality?

01-030-020   Make judgments about media by evaluating different presentations. VI

01-030-025   Use the techniques of mass media for persuading an audience. V

01-030-030   Describe the techniques of advertising and analyze its effects. IV

Index

Chemistry (*continued*)
  metric system (*see* Metric system)
  molecules (*see* Molecules)
  oxidation and reduction, SC-020-100
  pH (*see* pH)
  principal products, predicting, SC-020-125
  solids and liquids (*see* Solids and liquids)
  temperature (*see* Temperature)
  water (*see* Water)
  weight (*see* Weight)
  See also Matter
Children and young people
  development of child, SS-025-050
  juvenile delinquency, SS-010-170; SS-025-055
  literary works about, LA-025-155
  sexual attitudes, SS-025-060
  socialization, SS-020-045
China, SS-010-250; SS-015-060
  early civilization, SS-010-005
  economic development, SS-005-140; SS-010-185
  maps and globes, SS-015-010
  overpopulation, SS-010-250; SS-015-065, 070
  revisionism of Mao Tse-tung, SS-010-260
  totalitarianism, SS-010-200, 215, 220
Christianity
  Judeo-Christian ethics, SS-010-010
  Protestant Reformation, SS-010-015
  Roman Catholic Church, SS-010-015; SS-020-125
Circles, MA-015-015, 055; MA-030-005
  constructing and measuring, MA-015-020
  definitions and properties, MA-015-050; MA-020-015
  description and classification, MA-015-005, 010
  graphing relations and functions, MA-025-120
Cities, SS-005-030, 125; SS-020-140
  growth, SS-005-250, 265; SS-015-070; SS-020-145
  problems, SS-020-150, 155, 160
  rural and urban societies contrasted, SS-020-130, 135
  technology, SS-020-025
  See also Population concentration and growth
Civil rights
  censorship, SS-010-155
  Constitutional provisions, SS-010-055, 160, 170
  guns, sale of, SS-010-170
  limitations, SS-010-165
  See also Constitution, United States
Civil War (U.S.), SS-010-094, 140, 160
Class structure. *See* Social controls; Social problems
Climate. *See* Weather and climate
Clothing needs, SS-005-005
Clouds, SC-010-065